THE PSYCHEDELIC TEACHER

THE PSYCHEDELIC TEACHER

Drugs, Mysticism, and Schools

by IGNACIO L. GÖTZ

THE WESTMINSTER PRESS
Philadelphia

ISBN 0-664-20923-8 (cloth)

ISBN 0-664-24941-8 (paper)

LIBRARY OF CONGRESS CATALOG CARD NO. 75-183118

Grateful acknowledgment is made to *The New York Times* for permission to reprint "Surfing Has Become for Some a Way to Religious Experience," by Edward B. Fiske. © 1970 by The New York Times Company.

PUBLISHED BY THE WESTMINSTER PRESS ®
PHILADELPHIA, PENNSYLVANIA

PRINTED IN THE UNITED STATES OF AMERICA

For Katherine

It is easier to sail many thousand miles through cold and storm and cannibals, in a government ship, with five hundred men and boys to assist one, than it is to explore the private sea, the Atlantic and Pacific Ocean of one's being alone.
    —Thoreau, *Walden*

From the unreal lead me to the real!
    —*Brihad-Aranyaka Upanishad* 1.3.28

CONTENTS

PREFACE

I would like to preface this little book with a note of thanks to the many people who have rendered it possible in one way or another. Many of my students and friends have volunteered invaluable information and criticism from their own experience. They have taught me many things, and in their own way they have confirmed experientially many thoughts contained in these pages. My colleague, Dr. Mary Anne Raywid, was kind and patient enough to go over the first drafts, and helped me much by her pointed and insightful comments. My wife, Katherine, a constant sharer of ideas, found time away from her many household chores to review the manuscript at its various stages and to suggest numerous corrections. I am grateful to all of them, and I only hope that these pages bear, in some measure, the fruit of their labors.

I. L. G.

INTRODUCTION

Concern for drug use is widespread today in our country. Seminars and conferences are being organized to discuss the problem, legislation to counter the use is being proposed, legislators show their concern for "the drug crisis" as a means of proving to their constituencies how involved they are in the problems of the day, and so on. The instances of concern could be multiplied almost indefinitely.

Within this context I have noticed a very peculiar way of talking and writing about drugs today. Hardly anyone employs the word "use" in connection with drugs. Everything is "abuse." The impression I get from reading the current literature and listening to the countless programs on drugs that appear on radio and television is that legitimate use of drugs is unthinkable. It would seem that the judgment has already been rendered: drugs can *only* be "abused." This is the overall impression created. And this impression is derived even from some so-called expert literature and from Government reports. There are exceptions, of course. Geller and Boas have produced a good, accessible study,[1] and Marin and Cohen's book, *Understanding Drug Use: An Adult's Guide to Drugs and the Young,*[2] is even sympathetic and full of good sense and advice. Also, studies such as Barber's *LSD, Marijuana, Yoga, and Hypnosis,*[3] Hoffer and Osmond's *The Hallucinogens,*[4] Klüver's *Mescal and Mechanisms of Hallucinations*[5] (which reprints Klüver's classic study, first published in 1928, and long out of print and impossible to get), the collection edited by David E. Smith, *Drug Abuse Papers 1969,*[6] and many other scientific studies, offer a critical, unbiased approach to the subject. But these studies are hard to obtain and generally beyond the sphere of interest of most of us. What predominates and what ultimately shapes public opinion in this area is a hodgepodge of bias, ignorance, and myth.

Anyone who approaches a problem with his mind made up can hardly be expected to be fair-minded in his consideration of the problem. Persons for whom there is only drug "abuse" have, in fact, prejudged the issue even before it has been fully considered. It might be possible, indeed, to discover uses of drugs—even of mescaline and LSD—that would not be abusive. I am not talking only of drug use in medical and psychiatric therapy or in research. I have in mind here the kind of use that is moderate, guided, purposeful, and conducive to a change of character that we say we value. One of the main concerns of this short book will be to elucidate this point.

Now, if I object to the term "abuse" and prefer the

unbiased term "use," I should define as clearly and suc-
cinctly as possible my understanding of these terms. By
drug use I mean here the act or series of acts, self-initiated
or initiated by others, of employing drugs for any purpose
whatsoever, for instance, self-enlightenment, therapy, escape, social relaxation, and prompted by any motive whatsoever, such as the desire to explore the unknown, the urge
to flee from a harrowing situation, the pleasantness of
euphoria, sheer social conviviality, and so on. By drug
abuse I mean, following David E. Smith's definition, the
employment of drugs "to the point where it seriously in-
terferes with the individual's health or his economic or
social functioning." [7]

In this book I will consistently employ the term "drug
use," since any serious interference with an individual's
health or his economic and/or social functioning as a result of drugs is a matter to be demonstrated in every case,
not to be generally presumed. To do otherwise, it seems
to me, would involve prejudice.

Another point is worth mentioning. Although the arguments I will present will, to be truly and fully valid, have
to apply to *all* drug use—that is, to experiences produced
by all varieties of drugs—my main concern is going to be
centered around the psychedelics. In order to make this
distinction clear I have included a brief systematic classification of drugs in Appendix I. However, given the emphasis on the psychedelics, I think a few words about them
are in order here.

According to Hoffer and Osmond, hallucinogens are
"chemicals which in nontoxic doses produce changes in
perception, in thought, and in mood, but which seldom
produce mental confusion, memory loss, or disorientation
for person, place, and time. These latter changes are

characteristic of organic brain reactions following intoxica-
tions with alcohol, anaesthetic, and other toxic drugs." [8]

Hallucinogens are drugs such as LSD and mescaline,
which can enrich the mind and enlarge the vision, and
which sometimes trigger fantastic aesthetic experiences as
well as mystical experiences valued by the subjects above
all others. They also have definite potential for the exami-
nation of psychological disorders, for therapy, and for the
study of society, religion, and philosophy.[9]

The potential of the hallucinogens, as well as of other
drugs, cannot be denied by any fair-minded person. The
question, of course, is the kind of use to which the potential
is put. A matter of primary importance is not to prejudge
the issue. One must accept *all* the evidence, however un-
prepared one may be for what the evidence might bring.
And one must be ready to accept the conclusions, however
distasteful or self-incriminating they be. In short, one must
approach this problem of drugs with an open mind. Sure
enough, there are laws in existence in this country which
prohibit certain uses of certain drugs. The word "abuse"
may at times be used in this context of the law, to denote
illegality, and not necessarily inappropriateness.

This is, no doubt, the truth in some instances. But the
fact of the existence of laws must not be an obstacle to the
fair consideration of the total problem. Laws, after all, are
made to serve people, not to enslave them. Laws represent
the minimal standards of morality that a society which is
conscious of itself wishes to observe, and as these standards
change, so do the laws—at least in theory, and sometimes
reluctantly and belatedly. One has but to think of prohibi-
tion days, of "monkey trials" and trials for witchcraft, and
of McCarthyism's purges. The point is, simply, that within
the flexible and dynamic society the law can never be an

absolute and unchangeable standard. It is only the reflection of the consciousness of people in their pursuits and strivings.

Applied to the question at hand, this means that arguments with regard to the appropriateness or inappropriateness of drug use can never be validly foreclosed by an appeal to the law, for the law follows, rather than anticipates, the settling of the argument one way or another.

I offer these remarks here by way of introduction and in an effort to obtain a fair hearing. One of my main contentions is that we are approaching the problem of drug use with our minds so determinedly made up one way that we can hardly be expected to get an adequate view of the total situation. I believe that the arguments presented here dwell on substantially large aspects of this total situation, and that therefore they ought to be given serious consideration by anyone desiring to ameliorate society. I hope that the following pages will prove useful to everyone, but, above all, I hope that they will prove enlightening.

CHAPTER 1

The Drug Phenomenon as Symptom

Nothing is true that forces one to exclude.

—Camus, *The Myth of Sisyphus*

The phenomenon of drug use in our time is most interesting, puzzling, and disturbing. It is also one of the most exploited by the various information media. The chemistry of drugs, the way drugs influence consciousness and behavior, is a fascinating subject of study for physicians and psychologists. The description of the drug subculture is of prime interest for the sociologist. Anthropologists have devoted a lot of their time, often undergoing grave risks, in the study of the cultural effects of the drug experience among various peoples of the world. Religionists have compared the drug experience with the religious experience, and educationists have busied themselves with the ways of preventing the widespread use of drugs in their schools and in society at large. Finally, innumerable parents have been confronted with the anguishing questions that drug use raises in their own families.

The literature on drugs is enormous. Government publications describe the effects of drug use, inform prospective users of the laws and the penalties they prescribe, and advise of the various possible consequences, legal and medical, that may be visited on the drug user. Besides these short tracts, there exists a vast array of more scholarly publications, tracing the history of the use of various drugs in various societies, collecting literature from famous drug users the world over, and describing the various scientific researches that have been conducted. A smaller number of publications deal with drug uses in a wider sense, bringing in the religious and cultural connotations of the use, the esoteric significance attached to the experience, and even the cultic aspects of drugs.

Most of these publications, while correct in their varied stances, treat the drug experience as a social phenomenon that must be contended with. Moreover, nearly all publications, with few exceptions, are unabashedly opposed to the use of psychotropic drugs. They see in them only evil, an epidemic, a sickness unto death. The few exceptions usually content themselves with pointing to the therapeutic uses of LSD or the religious significance of the drug experience.

With regard to the goodness or badness, appropriateness or inappropriateness, of drug use I shall take a position later on when I discuss the religious significance of the drug experience. Here I want to make clear how this study differs methodologically from the others.

I do not intend to ignore the social significance of the drug movement. But rather than analyze it and describe it only from the purely medical or social-scientific point of view, I want to consider it from the vantage point of more cosmic and subjective impressions. In other words, I want to emphasize in this study what is usually neglected or de-emphasized in most studies, namely, the religious and transcendental meaning of the experience induced by drugs.

I will be dealing fully with the religious and transcendental aspects of the psychedelic experience later on. Here, lest the reader be turned off by the introduction of these terms into a discussion of the drug phenomenon, a preliminary explanation seems to be called for.

There is no doubt today among serious researchers that there *is* a transcendental or religious dimension to many drug-induced experiences. This stage of experience is encountered primarily, and almost exclusively, in experiences induced by hallucinogenic drugs such as LSD, mescaline, and psilocybin. Walter Pahnke, whose research in this field is outstanding, has shown that there is

> a specific form of psychedelic experience that is frequently reported when relatively high dosage is administered to normal subjects or selected mental patients in supportive settings. For want of a better term, we have called this form of experience *mystical consciousness*.[1]

In the early 1960's, Jean Houston, of the Foundation for Mind Research, conducted an investigation into the effects of LSD and other techniques and procedures designed to expand consciousness. This particular research revealed a pattern of deepening awareness consisting of four levels: the sensory, the psychological or ontogenetic, the phylogenetic, and the *mysterium*.

The phylogenetic level sees the subject recalling vividly myths and rituals of the race, either learned or experienced or in some fashion recalled from the collective experience of mankind, as the Jungian explanation would have it. But beyond this level is the mystical one, experienced or reached by fewer subjects and involving the confrontation with a *mysterium* that is sensed, almost always, as "the source level of reality." As Houston describes the experience,

> the semantics of theological discourse become visceral realities in the experiencing subject; the well-known concepts referring to a "primordial essence" or an "ultimate ground of being" take on an immediacy and directness hitherto unsuspected. . . . Another aspect of the experience is in the subject becoming aware of himself as continuous with the energy of the universe. It is frequently described with words to the effect that the subject was part of a dynamic continuum. It is also experienced as a state in which the subject professes to being filled by divinity. . . . The subject will experience the world as transfigured and unified. He will report himself to be caught up in an undifferentiated unity wherein the knower, the knowledge, and the known are experienced as a single reality.[2]

Such experiences, then, which I have called religious or transcendental, are, in fact, produced by the ingestion of certain quantities of psychedelic drugs. The evidence for this is clear and conclusive. The occurrence of such phenomena is a datum one must seek to interpret.

To be sure, individual drug users may blow their minds seemingly for a variety of reasons, and social workers as well as psychiatrists in our overcrowded cities are aware of those avowed reasons, and in fact can account for them better than I can. This is their job, and they perform it magnificently. Similarly, scientific researchers have been doing extremely good and interesting work in determining the chemical processes and therapeutic uses of the psychotropic drugs. It is therefore understandable—though not thereby totally justifiable: to understand is *not* to justify— that, caught in the anguish produced by the many incidents of alienation and drug addiction, such researchers and social workers should be predominantly, almost exclusively, concerned with the immediate prevention of drug abuse and with the treatment of those who do become addicted. When lives are ruined in front of our very eyes, our immediate concern is directed against the factors proximately responsible for such a calamity: the drugs themselves, the pushers, the peddlers. In such cases we worry about the addict and about his parents and relatives, we sympathize with their pain and their bewilderment, and we try to offer solace and remedy. When death occurs as the result of drug abuse a sense of urgency grips us, and we spring into action in ways that are often as misguided as they are well-meaning.

But the scientific, social, and medical aspects of drug use (as well as abuse) do not tell the whole story. There are aesthetic, metaphysic, and religious aspects as well. Ignorance of these aspects by the researcher is often due to his narrow specialization, and this one can understand, even if one finds it impossible to justify fully. But deliberate and willful neglect of the religious aspects is not only not understandable, it is unforgivable. It is unforgivable because it is a deliberate obliteration of one aspect of the truth of an event, one element of the data. It is unforgivable because it is hypocritical, because it pretends to take cognizance of the *whole* event while deliberately negating a part of it, because it maintains that it is giving the facts when, truly, it deliberately conceals aspects of these very facts.[3]

It should not be thought that these two states of ignorance and willful misinterpretation are the sole property of the unlettered. They can be found in the highest echelons of researchers and of Government officials. In November, 1963, in its final report, the President's Advisory Commission on Narcotic and Drug Abuse wrote:

> The Commission has received convincing evidence that a critical need exists for an extensive and enlightened educational effort on drug abuse. The problem is still clouded by misconceptions and misinformation. . . . These distorted attitudes are not confined to the general public; many fallacies continue to persist in professional circles. . . .
>
> Some of the public misconceptions stem from newspapers and magazines which have emphasized the more lurid aspects of drug abuse. Others can be traced to the romanticized writings of Coleridge, De Quincey and Aldous Huxley on the effects of drugs.[4]

It is obvious, however, that even if the writings of Huxley and others are "romanticized" accounts of experiences induced by drugs, such experiences have been found in every civilization of which there is record, and they have been consistently associated with a desire to transcend the bonds of ordinary reality. To dismiss this aspect of the drug-induced experience by labeling it "romanticized" is neither enlightened nor scientific.

Moreover, such unscientific narrow-mindedness contributes greatly to the widening of the credibility gap, and is basically at the root of the failure of most, if not all, current so-called drug education programs in this country. To the youth who have *experienced* LSD, Baudelaire, Coleridge, De Quincey, Huxley, and Leary are right, no matter what the Government says or what their teachers *say*. As psychologist Helen Nowlis puts it, such contention

> just doesn't correspond with the experience the kids are having. . . . It's a crazy imbalance to stress marijuana hallucinations when 99% of the kids who try a marijuana cigarette don't get hallucinations, and it may do serious harm. A lot of heroin users say, "You lied to us about pot—so we didn't believe you about heroin." [5]

In a way, the suspicion with which such Government reports are greeted reflects the attitude that many young Americans entertain toward politics and its insidious influence on all levels of life. Government reports that contradict, deny, obscure, suppress, or misrepresent the facts are thought to reflect political influences, pressures, and advantages, and not the result of unbiased research and the concern for truth. There are exceptions, of course. But one has only to reflect on Congressional reactions to, for instance, the recent report on marijuana prepared by the National Institute of Mental Health in order to realize that political expediency, not concern for facts, determines most Government statements on this (and other) subjects. In the State of California marijuana has been officially classed as a narcotic when, from the point of view of pharmacology, this classification is erroneous. And what is one to think of the official concern about drug addiction, which usually reflects interest in addiction to narcotics (primarily heroin), when in the United States alone 1 person in 4,000 is a heroin addict, while 1 out of 20 Americans is an alcoholic? Who thinks of alcohol as a drug? And who has forgotten the protracted fights to ban the advertisements, on radio and television at least, of the drug nicotine? There is really no reason to suppose that Government-sponsored drug research has not, and will not, be jaundiced by political astuteness. Politicians do not seem to be concerned with the historical fact that "no society can long afford to be dishonest." [6]

But besides the emphasis on the metaphysical and religious aspect of the drug-induced experience, there is another methodological point I must state now. This point is crucial and distinctive to this study, and I hope I can make its meaning clear. I intend to treat the phenomenon of drug use *as a symptom,* that is, as a sign or indication of an underlying event that one may call cause. The sense of this statement is clear, I am sure, to the psychiatrist and the social worker. The "mixed-up kid" who has deep identity problems or comes from a broken home or an abnormal family situation is likely to end up mainlining heroin. In such an instance, the youngster's bewilderment and yearning for release from his troublesome situation causes him to use drugs as a means of escape. Drug use, or even addiction, in his case, is a symptom of an underlying malaise.

In calling drug use symptomatic, or in treating it as a symptom, I am implying that *all* drug use is causally connected with an underlying factor, the same in all instances. I am implying, and will seek to prove, that there is a common denominator to all drug use, and that this common denominator must be viewed as the causative factor of the use. Even though, as I have stated earlier, I will be primarily concerned with the use of hallucinogenic drugs, I must make it clear that the arguments presented here apply to *all* drug use.

Let me explain this further. Since the time of Hume one of the ways of speaking about causal connection is to understand it as a three-term relationship. This means that one can say that A causes B whenever B invariably follows from A under circumstances of kind C. The question, of course, entails knowledge and control of C sufficient to vary it and thus determine if B still invariably follows A.[7] Whenever the conditions are verified, if B invariably follows A, one can say that B is an effect of A. One can also say that B is a symptom of A, that is, that whenever B is present, A must have preceded. It is in this sense that I am calling drug use symptomatic.

There are several reasons why I want to treat drug use as symptomatic. In the first place, I want to do so because I am convinced I can verily show that drug use *is* symptomatic. Secondly, because if drug use is symptomatic, it makes very little sense to expend all one's energies and resources treating the symptom without doing anything about its causes. Yet this seems to be the current pattern of reaction to drug use. There are exceptions, of course, such as the Federal Government's Drug Abuse Education Act of 1970 (P.L. 91-527), where, in Sec. 4, one reads that the "primary emphasis" of the programs should be on the "treatment of causes rather than symptoms." This attitude, however, so far is the exception rather than the rule. In fact, the situation is similar to that of a physician who continues to administer morphine to a patient suffering from acute appendicitis, without ever bothering to operate. To hope for a cure in such a case is wishful thinking with a vengeance. It is like the rhyme that children sing when rain comes to spoil their happy outing: "Rain, rain, go away, come again another day!" Unless we do something about the weather, there is going to be more rain.

There is yet a third reason. Maybe we do not want to do away altogether with the rain. Maybe what we want is to control the weather in such ways that rains won't be destructive, or that climates won't be rainy all the time. Or maybe other circumstances need to be changed. In India, when the monsoon season comes, it rains as if rain were going out of style. The rivers swell up, and, leaving a trail of misery and destruction, they quickly empty all that water into the sea. Ah, if there were but ways of conserving some of that water for the dry months ahead, when not a raindrop falls and the earth becomes parched and cracked and sterile! All that rainwater could be stored in reservoirs and then released through various canals. It is the same with drug use when viewed as symptomatic. The use of drugs may simply be a sign that, in our present-day society, the underlying cause of the symptom has been given only one course through which to empty out its energy. But there may be other ways to release the pressure. The question, then, is one of channeling such release. This is a question I shall seek to clarify in Chapter 3.

At this point I should return to my claim that drug use is symptomatic and endeavor to explain what it is symptomatic of. In a general sense, drug use is symptomatic of, or caused by, a deep underlying concern and search for values and experiences that may render human life meaningful. This is the main thesis I have to substantiate. I see drug use today, especially among the young, as the symptom of a fundamental concern for the meaning and value of human life. As William Braden has put it:

People have started once more to ask ultimate questions. They are asking who they are, and who God is, and what is the relationship, if any, between them and him. Altizer is asking these questions, and so is the hipster who seeks cosmic fireworks in an LSD sugar cube.[8]

This means, really, that a basic causative factor of the phenomenon of drug use is to be found in the search for ultimate answers prompted by the lack of cohesion in our social life today. Durkheim, for instance, saw as one of the most important functions of religion to provide integrating experiences, guiding norms, by which to avoid the tendencies to anomie and alienation in society.[9] As Thomas Cosgriff has expressed it, part of the explanation of drug use among the young

lies in the feeling of uselessness that many young persons have in a society which allows them no serious role, and disparages young and old alike. Another factor is the reaction of the young to the shallow, hypocritical existence which seems to envelop them. They can no longer be sure of values when all values are held up to a critical scrutiny. Like the people in the slums, they exist in a state of anomie, only not social so much as moral and ethical. Their dilemma brings to mind the question of Kant: "What can I know?" "What ought I to do?" "What may I hope?" [10]

Theodore Roszak is basically correct when he sees the youth "counter culture" developing today as essentially "an exploration of the politics of consciousness." [11] The concern is, of course, far more pervasive, and the drug phenomenon is but one symptom of this deep-seated urge. Put differently, this is tantamount to saying that in the pursuit of deeper meanings and ultimate understanding, the use of drugs is but one means toward the end of fuller consciousness. As Stace has suggested, it is "evidently a fact that such an experience, momentary though it may be, can in some way illuminate with permanent and lasting happiness, peace, and satisfaction a life which was previously dark with despair." [12] Research has amply substantiated this. A classic aspect of the drug experience is the intimation of broader perspectives, "the sudden insight that one has been living in a narrow space-time-self context." [13] With this objective in mind—which, incidentally, has been one objective of drug use over the centuries—why should drugs not be used, in Roszak's words, "as a kind of psychic depth charge with which to open up courses of perception that have become severely log-jammed due to the entrenched cerebral habits of our Western intelligence?" [14] For, as Camus would add, "to a man devoid of blinders, there is no finer sight than that of the intelligence at grips with a reality that transcends it." [15]

William James, writing about "the consciousness produced by intoxicants and anaesthetics, especially by alcohol," has this to say:

> The sway of alcohol over mankind is unquestionably due to its power to stimulate the mystical faculties of human nature, usually crushed to earth by the cold facts and dry criticisms of the sober hour. Sobriety diminishes, discriminates, and says no; drunkenness expands, unites, and says yes. It is in fact the great exciter of the *Yes* function in man. It brings its votary from the chill periphery of things to the radiant core. It makes him for the moment one with truth. Not through mere perversity do men run after it. To the poor and the unlettered it stands in the place of sym-

phony concerts and of literature; and it is part of the deeper mystery and tragedy of life that whiffs and gleams of something that we immediately recognize as excellent should be vouchsafed to so many of us only in the fleeting earlier phases of what in its totality is so degrading a poisoning. The drunken consciousness is one bit of the mystic consciousness, and our total opinion of it must find its place in our opinion of that larger whole.

Nitrous oxide and ether, especially nitrous oxide, when sufficiently diluted with air, stimulate the mystical consciousness in an extraordinary degree Depth beyond depth of truth seems revealed to the inhaler. This truth fades out, however, or escapes, at the moment of coming to; and if any words remain over in which it seemed to clothe itself, they prove to be the veriest nonsense. Nevertheless, the sense of a profound meaning having been there persists, and I know more than one person who is persuaded that in the nitrous oxide trance we have a genuine metaphysical revelation.[16]

This being the case, the remarks, heard in high Government circles, that mankind has always frowned on the use of alcohol and other hallucinogenics, must be understood either as an exaggeration or as the result of ignorance. To be sure, certain behaviors have always been frowned upon in various societies. An important question to ask, however, is *why* this has happened, and what kinds of behavior have been frowned upon. Socrates' contemporaries, for instance, obviously did not relish his inquisitive behavior. As far as drugs are concerned, perhaps one reason for objection has been the confusion between use and abuse—after all, even James calls the "totality" of drunkenness a degrading poisoning. I think it would be correct to say that certain abusive behaviors have, in fact, been frowned upon. But it would be unwarranted to say that *all use* has been so castigated, much less to assert that all use is *ipso facto* abuse. A good example of this confusion between use and abuse can be seen in the report, alluded to above, of the President's Advisory Commission on Narcotic and Drug *Abuse*. The very title suggests that the Commission was not even concerned with whether or not drug use was always abusive: it assumed so. Its mind was made up even before it inquired into the phenomenon. Further evidence of this is even clearer in the body of the report. According to the Commission, whoever uses drugs must be either sick, with some "personality disturbance," or a juvenile delinquent. A less scientific and unbiased attitude can hardly be envisioned.

Furthermore, one must judiciously ask what is the demarcating line between use and abuse. And in establishing this distinction it must never be forgotten that in all societies of which there is record there has been a certain fear of knowing oneself and one's universe too well. In fact, there was a time during the first half of this century of enlightenment when many philosophers maintained that the very question "What am I?" was meaningless and ought not to be asked. As Alan Watts remarks, "the most strongly enforced of all known taboos is the taboo against knowing who or what you really are behind the mask of your apparently separate, independent, and isolated ego." [17] Hence the esoteric character of all doctrines and sects that claimed to help the individual discover his true identity. Against this background it would be simply foolish not to ask ourselves, before making a final judgment on the current drug phenomenon, whether or not our ready condemnation of drug use is not, in some way, the expression of the ancient taboo against knowing oneself. Not without reason was Socrates' death an enactment of this taboo, since he was committed to the proposition that the unexamined life is not worth living.

But if ultimate concerns are the general underlying cause of drug use, the concern for religious values and religious experiences of some sort is a more specific or particular cause. I use words carefully here. I do not mean to imply that there is today, among our youth, a deep-seated concern for *religion*. Rather, the concern must be for *experiences* that can be qualitatively classified as religious. What I have in mind here is that kind of experience in which, as Jean Houston notes, there is a confrontation with a *mysterium,* or that level of experience which Pahnke calls mystical consciousness, the seer's ecstasy and its description in a literature that is clearly identifiable in the religious tradition of mankind. This distinction between *religion* and the *religious* is not a new one, though it is largely ignored by most writers. The classical formulations are to be found in Schleiermacher's *On Religion,* in Rudolf Otto's *The Idea of the Holy,* and in John Dewey's *A Common Faith.*

Later on I shall take pains to describe and identify the religious experience as distinct from other experiences, aesthetic, for instance, and intellectual. In terms of drug-induced experiences this distinction is well explained in the work of Pahnke, Houston, and others. The important thing to remember here is that ultimate concerns play themselves out at two different levels, the experiential and the conceptual. Religion, with its dogmas and explanations, with its institutions and structures, is a product of the conceptual. So is philosophy when it constructs a system that hangs together logically. But such concepts as may appear in philosophy and religion have been applied to "something" experienced by the conceptualizer. When we try to understand a momentous experience that we have undergone, we use concepts with which we are more or less familiar: we compare, contrast, analyze, in terms of the conceptual generalizations we have obtained from other experiences, within the context of the culture in which we have grown up. This process is also operative in the effort to explain to someone else what *we* have experienced. But all along, the experience is primary both in a temporal order and in importance. This appears clearly in the case of the religious history of mankind, a fact that prompted Jung to see present-day religious concerns as embedded in the collective unconscious.[18]

The primacy of experience, where experience occurs, makes it possible to understand why the experience is always described as "ineffable" in its complexity and totality. Parts of it may be expressed, conceptualized, conveyed one way or another, even in very inadequate ways, but the inner core remains incommunicable. This also explains why the impact of the experience, its meaning, the "feeling" of it, remains often beyond the blurring of concepts and the forgetfulness of words. Conversely, the lack of a prior experience often renders meaningless the conceptual and institutional apparatus that is organized religion and systematic philosophy. Dogma, ritual, and theology appear empty to the one who has had no religious or metaphysical experience to fill it. In their inability to allow for and foster this experiential dimension Western religions and philosophies have miserably failed man.[19]

As a point of historical confirmation, it is interesting to note that the great intellectual genius of Aquinas suddenly dried up midway through the writing of the third part of the *Summa,* which he never completed. When the faithful

Brother Reginald urged him to continue, Thomas answered, "I can't because all that I have written seems like chaff to me." [20] A similar apologetic disclaimer is found in Plato:

> Thus much, at least, I can say about all writers, past or future, who say they know the things to which I devote myself. . . . There neither is nor ever will be a treatise of mine on the subject. For it does not admit of exposition like other branches of knowledge. . . . If they had appeared to me to admit adequately of writing and exposition, what task in life could I have performed nobler than this, to write what is of great service to mankind and to bring the nature of things into the light for all to see? [21]

But this is not all. What I have said about conceptualization in religion and philosophy is true also of the technologized society in which we live. I am not in any way insinuating that technology is wrong, just as I would not claim that theology and systematic philosophy are wrong and useless. The question here is one of preponderant emphasis. What I am decrying is the conceptual emphasis that often aggrandizes itself to the point where it forgets its experiential origins. That this is so in philosophy, in religion, and even in the arts (what else are the blips, whooshes, and squiggles that buzz out of synthesizers but conceptual schemes, Menotti's Globolinks), is, I think, undeniable. But this is equally so in technology and in very many of the social structures built upon it.[22]

One outstanding example of this overconceptualization has been the establishment (in the First Amendment's sense of the term [23]) of a so-called neutral system of education whose main effect has been, precisely, the enhance-

ment of the conceptual and the scientific to the neglect of
the experiential and valuational. I do not want to belabor
the point here, since I shall return to it in Chapter 3, but
I think it is of paramount importance to see the use of
drugs today as *a means* of breaking loose from the clasps
of the conceptual and the technical, from "the system," in
an effort to experience the wholeness of life, and in the
hope thereby of finding meaning and purpose in human
existence. As Osmond has put it:

> I believe that the psychedelics provide a chance, per-
> haps only a slender one, for homofaber, the cunning,
> ruthless, foolhardy, pleasure-greedy toolmaker, to
> emerge into that other creature whose presence we
> have so rashly presumed, homo sapiens, the wise,
> the understanding, the compassionate, in whose four-
> fold vision . . . art, politics, science and religion
> are one. Surely we must seize the chance.[24]

In this light, drug use today must be seen as a stage of the
movement, already in vogue for some time, in which ad-
venturous spirits have sought relevant meaning and religious categories in the religious traditions of the East,
where the importance of mysticism and the religious experience has been maintained more definite and unadul-
terated. This is one reason, again, for the symptomatic
nature of the phenomenon of interest in Oriental religions.
That is why so many of our youth

> read ancient Hindu sages, the *I Ching,* the *Tibetan
> Book of the Dead.* . . . The mystical lore of the
> East serves as a guide through this virgin terrain.
> . . . Their faith reposes in astrologer's charts, gurus,
> and an uncompromising commitment "to know thy-
> self." A subsequent preoccupation with the East—
> especially India—has led to the popularity of the

meditative retreats known as ashrams, Yoga disciplines, and Hare [sic!] Krishna chants as the more efficacious means of restoring the psyche to an atmosphere of contemplative calm.[25]

Of course, the claim that *all* drug use without exception is a symptom of a transcendental quest would seem highly questionable at first sight. In the first place, not all use of hallucinogenics leads to experiences that can be adequately classified as mystical. We know enough about the various dimensions or levels of experience produced by varying dosages of hallucinogenics to feel sure that the deepest ecstatic levels are not always reached. Pahnke stresses the fact that "many experimental subjects who have only seen visionary imagery and felt powerful emotions may be understood to have had nonmystical experiences of an aesthetic, psychoanalytic, or psychotic nature." In fact, he suggests, "the experiences of most people at 'LSD parties' are of an aesthetic nature." [26]

Moreover, not all drugs produce the kinds of experiences primarily associated with the mystical consciousness. Such experiences are produced by the psychedelics, and by other drugs only in more or less exceptional circumstances (such as obtain in the delirium tremens of alcoholics). Further, one can raise serious doubts about the claim that drug use is symptomatic of a religious quest when one takes cognizance of the pitiable states induced by heroin and opium addiction. Is the mugger who desperately needs money to support his habit a seeker of enlightenment? Is this a serious claim? Finally, there is the seeming light-headedness of many drug users for whom the drug experience is simply a matter of fad or peer pressure, youth's equivalent of their parents' urge "to keep up with the Joneses."

Despite all these reasonable objections, my claim is that drug use is revelatory of a deep unrest about the meaning of life, of a striving for purpose and ideals, something to live for. It can be said that all men, as they mature, in their desire to unify (in some ways), to synthesize their experiences, in their search for completeness and identity, exhibit some kind of metaphysical (in the original, Greek sense) interest, a questioning that goes beyond the scientifically observable, objectifiable, quantifiable aspects of human experience.[27]

The call for completeness that we all have heard at some point in our lives, the search for identity that we all have experienced as we grew up, may unfold itself in various ways. Yet the starting point is the same. For some, because of favorable conditions, this search eventuates in holistic experiences, profound and deeply stirring insights of a religious or metaphysical nature, through which they find themselves and possess themselves unalterably. For others, because of less favorable conditions, the search reaches only the heights of aesthetic enjoyment and artistic self-realization, a step short, as it were, of the fuller synthesis. Others, still, because of unfavorable circumstances, because of overpowering inner and outer confusions and pressures, seek only to numb the poignant urge to find themselves, and to establish their place in their immediate milieu and in the universe at large. The numbing may be temporary and it may be transcended. Many of us tarry here and there before eventually proceeding in our quest for vision. Like Hesse's Siddhartha we endure long sojourns in samsara (that is, "the world"). But for many, the numbness is permanent. Yet, from the point of view of the search for identity, meaning, synthesis, even the heroin addict can be truly said to have felt, in some way, at some time, "the intimations of immortality." This experience, as causative of later symptoms, should not be neglected in favor of more immediate, more glamorous and newsworthy occurrences proximately connected with the use of heroin and the possible eventual addiction.

The general concern with the wholeness of life, with its metaphysical and religious connotations, need not be consciously expressed, though it is often so expressed, and we fail to appreciate the significance of such statements as we may come across because of our lack of human perspective or the semantics involved. But this purpose *is* often deliberately and consciously expressed. I have met young men who declared they had started to smoke pot out of a desire "to see God." Timothy Leary, of course, has advocated the use of LSD as a "sacrament," that is, a means of turning on to the religious dimensions of existence. Without necessarily agreeing with Leary on the universality of this sacramental use of LSD, I am contending here that drug use is a symptom regardless of explicitness or implicitness. Nay, more. The very fact that the religious concern is often not deliberate is more surely indicative of the symptomatic nature of the drug experience, for it diminishes the risk of fraud and deceit.

To conclude and summarize, I must emphasize once more the meaning and purpose of seeing drug use as symptomatic. I have already indicated that in treating drug use as symptomatic of an underlying concern for meaning and value I am maintaining that it is not enough to treat the symptom: the connection between the symptom and its cause must be accurately diagnosed, and only then can one intelligently decide what to do. If this is true, one must also conclude that it is possible, because of one's ignorance of the causal connection, to use the wrong

day we do not even suspect the depths of our inhumanity. Conversely, the immensity of our human potential may be dying without ever having been born. The symptoms are there, if we only knew them as symptoms.

In our culture, drug use is one such symptom. I have maintained so far that the drug experience, so widespread among youth today, is, in a general sense, symptomatic of an underlying concern for values, meaning, completeness in the outlook on life. I have also indicated that, specifically, this general concern appears to me to center around, or seeks its fulfillment in, experiences that are truly religious in nature. I have also claimed that this is so even though, often, there is no deliberate, explicit avowal of this purpose among drug users. Now I have to explain these claims further and substantiate them in detailed fashion.

The claim that the use of drugs is symptomatic of an underlying concern can be substantiated only if it can be shown convincingly that drugs are just one of a number of means (such as fasting, penances, contemplation, yoga, etc.) that can be used—and have, in fact, been used—in the search for ultimate meaning and, specifically, religious experiences and metaphysical illuminations. Moreover, one would have to show that such a search for ultimate categories of meaning is itself symptomatic of a deep-seated human instinct for wholeness and synthesis vis-à-vis man and the universe. The basic line of argument therefore will be as follows: (1) The psychedelic drug experience itself, from a descriptive and subjective point of view, is the same as the religious or mystical experience; (2) the human need for experiences that qualify as religious is a well-established fact; (3) the current generation has been denied the possibilities of this experience by the emphases on the secular as well as on the scientific aspects of our culture. These are the points I shall now proceed to substantiate.

1. THE DRUG EXPERIENCE AND THE RELIGIOUS EXPERIENCE

As I have stated above, the first part of this argument must seek to show that the experience induced by drugs is basically the same as the experience or experiences induced by, say, contemplation, mortification, fasts, yoga exercises, and the like. This is tantamount to saying that the experience induced by drugs is basically the same as a religious experience induced by other means.

The logical basis for this argument is clearly stated by Stace as follows:

> The principle of casual indifference is this: If X has an alleged mystical experience P_1 and Y has an alleged mystical experience P_2, and if the phenomenological characteristics of P_1 entirely resemble the phenomenological characteristics of P_2 so far as can be ascertained from the descriptions given by X and Y, then the two experiences cannot be regarded as being of two different kinds—for example, it cannot be said that one is a "genuine" mystical experience while the other is not—merely because they arise from dissimilar causal conditions.

> The principle seems logically self-evident. . . . It is introduced here because it is sometimes asserted that mystical experiences can be induced by drugs, such as mescaline, lysergic acid, etc. On the other hand, those who have achieved mystical states as a result of long and arduous spiritual exercises, fasting and prayer, or great moral efforts, possibly spread over many years, are inclined to deny that a drug can in-

duce a "genuine" mystical experience, or at least to
look askance at such practices and such a claim. Our
principle says that *if* the phenomenological descriptions of the two experiences are indistinguishable, so
far as can be ascertained, then it cannot be denied
that if one is a genuine mystical experience the other
is also. This will follow notwithstanding the lowly
antecedents of one of them, and in spite of the understandable annoyance of an ascetic, a saint, or a
spiritual hero, who is told that his careless and
worldly neighbour, who never did anything to deserve it, has attained to mystical consciousness by
swallowing a pill.[2]

I must now attempt to show, in accordance with this argument, that the phenomenological descriptions of such experiences entirely resemble one another. Compare the following passages:

I

Then . . . the Master . . . revealed to [X] his
transcendent, divine Form, speaking from innumerable mouths, seeing with a myriad eyes, of many
marvelous aspects, adorned with countless divine or-
naments, brandishing all kinds of heavenly weapons,
wearing celestial garlands and the raiment of paradise, anointed with perfumes of heavenly fragrance,
full of revelations, resplendent, boundless, of ubiquitous regard.

Suppose a thousands suns should rise together into
the sky: such is the glory of the shape of Infinite
God.

Then [X] beheld the entire universe, in all its multi-
tudinous diversity, lodged as one being within the
body of God. . . . Then was [X] . . . overcome

with wonder. His hair stood erect. He bowed low before God in adoration, and clasped his hands.

II

I continued to look at the flowers, and in their living light I seemed to detect the qualitative equivalent of breathing—but of breathing without return to a starting point, with no recurrent ebbs but only a repeated flow from beauty to heightened beauty, from deeper to ever deeper meaning. . . . My eyes travelled from the rose to the carnation, and from that feathery incandescence to the smooth scrolls of sentient amethyst which were the iris. The Beatific Vision, *Sat Chit Ananda,* Being-Awareness-Bliss—for the first time I understood, not only on the verbal level, not by inchoate hints or at a distance, but precisely and completely what those prodigious syllables referred to.

III

One time he was going out of devotion to a church . . . and the way went along by the river; and proceeding thus with his devotions, he sat down for awhile facing the river which flowed down below. While he was seated there the eyes of his understanding began to open; not that he saw a vision, but understanding and coming to know many things, both spiritual things and matters of faith and letters, too; the illumination was so great that everything seemed to him new. The particular details that he saw then are beyond narrating, although there were a great many, but he can only say that he received a great illumination of the understanding. So that in the whole course of his life, after sixty-two years, considering all the helps he has received from God and all the knowledge that has been his, even though you add all together, they do not seem to amount to what he received that one time alone.

IV

Despite of myself, my eyes remained fixed on an image which represented Christ with his heart offered for mankind. This picture hung on the wall of a church to which I had retired to pray. . . .

While I let my eyes wander over the picture, suddenly it seemed to me as if the contours of the image dissolved, faded away, and this, indeed, in a very special way, very difficult to describe. As I endeavoured to contemplate the contours of the image of the person of Christ, the folds of his dress, the radiance of his head, the brightness of his countenance . . . a transformation suddenly took place: everything seemed to loosen up, to get mixed together, without, however, disappearing altogether. The contours, the boundaries which separated Christ from the surrounding world, changed into a vibrating layer within which all differences ran into each other.

It seemed to me that the transformation affected at first only one definite portion of the outlines of the image, and that from there it spread outwards, till it encompassed the entire outline.

From that moment on the metamorphosis developed at a quicker pace, till it affected all things on earth.

In the beginning I noticed that the vibrant atmosphere, the halo around Christ, was no longer confined within limits, but radiated out into the limitless . . . right up to the remotest spheres of matter . . . the whole universe vibrated.

And yet, when I sought to single out the objects, I discovered them still as clearly delineated, as individualized as they had been before.

This entire outward movement that shone out from Christ proceeded especially from his heart. So I tried to go up-stream to this source, there to get hold of the rhythm. Accordingly, I turned my eyes again to the image, and at that moment the vision reached its culminating point. From Christ's motionless countenance an ineffable display of all the colors and lights of beauty was coming forth. Infinite variations of perfection melted into each other and blended into a harmony that fully satiated me. Behind this surface in motion, the incommunicable beauty of Christ flowed evenly and raised everything to a superior degree of unity.

This beauty of Christ I divined rather than perceived, for whenever I tried to pierce the layer of beauties in the foreground, there appeared other singular beauties which veiled once more the one true beauty, though somehow they still allowed an inkling of it.

V

A great Being or Power was traveling through the sky, his foot was on a kind of lightning as a wheel is on a rail, it was his pathway. The lightning was made entirely of the spirits of innumerable people close to one another, and I was one of them. He moved in a straight line, and each part of the streak or flash came into its short conscious existence only that he might travel. I seemed to be directly under the foot of God, and I thought he was grinding his own life up out of my pain. Then I saw that what he had been trying with all his might to do was to *change his course,* to *bend* the line of lightning to which he was tied, in the direction in which he wanted to go. I felt my flexibility and helplessness, and knew that he would succeed. He bended me, turning his corner by means of my hurt, hurting me more than I had ever been hurt in my life, and at the acutest point of this, as he passed, I saw. I understood for a moment things that I have now forgotten, things that no one could remember while retaining sanity. The angle was an obtuse angle, and I remember thinking . . . that had he made it a right or acute angle, I should have both suffered and "seen" more, and should probably have died.

He went on. . . . In that moment the whole of my life passed and I *understood* then. *This* was what it had all meant, *this* was the piece of work it had all been contributing to do. I did not see God's purpose, I only saw his intentness and his entire relentlessness towards his means. He thought no more of me than a man thinks of hurting a cork when he is opening wine, or hurting a cartridge when he is firing. And yet . . . my first feeling was, and it came with tears, "Domine non sum digna," for I had been lifted into a position for which I was too small. I realized that in that half hour . . . I had served God more distinctly and purely than I had ever done in my life before, or than I am capable of desiring to do. I was the means of his achieving and revealing something.

VI

I saw face to face at last.

Light streamed down from the sky such as I have never beheld. The sun shone with a new light, as though translucent gold were at its heart. I saw not only the physical sun but the spiritual sun also, which poured down on me as I walked in the garden. . . . The wonder was beyond anything I have ever read or imagined or heard men speak about. I was Adam walking alone in the first Paradise. . . .

Every flower spoke to me, every spider wove a miracle of intricacy for my eyes, every bird understood that here was Heaven come to earth. . . .

But there was something more wonderful than the Light within the light—more wonderful than the standstill of time. It was that God walked with me in the Garden as He did before the Fall. Whether I sat, whether I walked, He was there—radiant, burningly pure, holy beyond holy. When I breathed, I breathed Him; when I asked a question He both asked and answered it.

The preceding passages span a period of some two thousand years. They represent Eastern as well as Western experiences, male as well as female, drug induced as well as "spontaneous." The religious quality is unmistakable in all of them, and in terms of the criteria usually established for judging the genuineness of mystical experiences, it is impossible to extricate the drug-induced ones from the others.[3]

The first one is the famous vision of Sri Krishna's universal form, granted to Arjuna the warrior in the battlefield of Kurukshetra. It is found in the *Bhagavad-Gîtâ* xi. 9–14.[4] The second one is part of Aldous Huxley's experience under the influence of mescaline.[5] The third one is Ignatius Loyola's vision by the river Cardoner, in Spain.[6] The fourth one is the narrative of Pierre Teilhard de Chardin's own experience.[7] The fifth one is the ether-induced experience of an anonymous woman, and is to be found in William James's *The Varieties of Religious Experience*.[8] The sixth one is from Katharine Trevelyan's autobiography.[9]

Descriptively, from the point of view of their phenomenological content, these experiences are all similar. But one must inquire more deeply into this similarity. We must ask whether there are any characteristic common elements in these (as well as other similar) experiences and narratives, so that we may describe the kind of experience called religious and see how it encompasses drug-induced as well as other religious experiences. The search for common elements is important, for such elements or characteristics can be used as criteria for religious experiences, whether spontaneous or induced by drugs or other means.

Two things should be noted here. First of all, the determination of such criteria has already been made in numerous studies, and it has been accomplished by reference, primarily and almost exclusively, to the religious experience in the traditional sense of the term. This point is important, for it allows us to use the criteria with reference to both drug-induced and traditionally induced experiences without falling into a vicious circle. Secondly, one should note that criteria of religious experience have been in existence in all religious traditions since time immemorial. Sometimes they have been formulated in simple, naturalistic terms—"this is the way of Light, this is the way of Darkness"—but as sophistication has developed, they have often become intricate and extensive.

The most general characteristic of the religious experience is *reverence,* a complex sentiment or emotion involving wonder, fear, gratitude, humility.[10] These emotional reactions encompass, as we shall see, the fundamental aspects that have been diagnosed as religious, and they constitute, together, what one may call "the master sentiment" of religious experience.[11]

More specifically, the characteristics of a religious experience can be summarized in Rudolf Otto's formula, *mysterium tremendum,* the "mystery tremendous." The term *mysterium* denotes here a substantive content, while *tremendum* brings out the adjectival description of the experience.

What is implied by the term *mysterium?* First of all, says Otto, the experience of *something wholly other,* beyond understanding, beyond naming, beyond reach. Hence the terms usually associated with the experience: transcendent, *super*-natural, *super*-human. Secondly, the experienced other attracts, draws one to it, mesmerizes, *fascinates*—with the rich connotation this term brings. The mystery, writes Otto,

> may appear to the mind an object of horror and dread, but at the same time it is no less something that allures with a potent charm, and the creature, who trembles before it, utterly cowed and cast down, has always at the same time the impulse to turn to it, nay even to make it somehow his own. The "mystery" is for him not merely something to be wondered at but something that entrances him; and beside that in it which bewilders and confounds, he feels something that captivates and transports him with a strange ravishment.[12]

The third element or feeling is that of *exhilaration,* complete unutterable joy,[13] which often leads to a feeling or awareness of security, of salvation.[14]

The *tremendum,* first of all, encompasses the feeling of *awe,* that is, dread, a sense of the uncanny similar to the shiver down the spine that one experiences when first reading Poe's "The Raven." Secondly, there is the feeling of *majesty,* of overpoweringness, which often leads to a sense of negative self-feeling or humility.[15] Finally, there is the feeling or awareness of *energy,* of pulsating life, of possessiveness. Such are the main characters of a religious experience as described by Otto, and I basically agree with his description.

This set of characteristics or criteria, however, is by no means the only one in use. Stace proposes two sets of seven criteria for a mystical experience,[16] Spinks proposes five,[17] and James enumerates four, namely, ineffability, noetic quality, transiency, and passivity.[18] Joachim Wach, following James, proposes four: ultimacy of the experienced, totality of human response, intensity, and practical life commitment.[19] Finally, Pahnke, as prelude to the "Good Friday" experiment, adopted nine interrelated categories from a survey of the literature, relying especially on James and Stace. His criteria are:

1. Unity
2. Objectivity and reality
3. Transcendence of space and time
4. Sense of sacredness
5. Deeply felt positive mood
6. Paradoxicality
7. Alleged ineffability
8. Transiency
9. Positive changes in attitude and/or behavior.[20]

The need for such criteria arises at two levels. One is the level of simple phenomenological characteristics in which some experiences are classed as religious and others as nonreligious, depending on the descriptive content as avowed for by the subject. The other level is the argumentative one, in which one seeks to show that certain experiences are, indeed, religious, if they meet certain criteria, even though some people may strongly object. For depending on the set of criteria used, it is obvious that some experiences, whether spontaneous or induced, and whether induced by drugs or through other practices, will be characterized as religious, while other experiences will be discounted. The question whether or not drug-induced experiences are the same as traditionally classed religious experiences cannot be settled in the abstract but only in reference to a specified set of criteria that have been validly established as representative of what is generally, traditionally, termed and accepted as religious experience. It is this second argumentative level which Stace has in mind when formulating the principle of causal indifference quoted above.

At the level of simple phenomenological description no great problem arises beyond the problems of careful analysis and correlation. Even in a quick application of Otto's criteria to the samples quoted above, it easily becomes clear that, in varying degrees or emphases, one does find in them elements of transcendence, fascination, the feeling of exhilaration and joy, awe, majesty, humility, and a sense of energy, dynamism—a feeling akin to that which one has when one dives through a huge breaking wave,[21] or when one rides a horse without a saddle, or when one revs up the powerful engine of a motorcycle or an automobile.

But things are not as simple at the argumentative level. One could, of course, insist on the validity of the argument presented by Stace, but even in such a case the question can always be raised, Are the experiences, in fact, indistinguishable? Stace himself recognizes the problem, but thinks that to date there is no conclusive argument either way. The problem arises simply because one can always question the appropriateness of any set of criteria, even though the ones here presented are generally accepted as valid by writers on the subject.

This problem has been hotly debated in the past. It has often been stated in terms of the distinction between so-called *natural* mysticism and *theistic* mysticism. The question is not raised solely with reference to drug-induced experiences, since from time immemorial there have been persons who could somehow "commune" with nature, and who even experienced a rapture similar in many respects to the trances of the religious mystics.

In some respects, this problem is one of ultimate assumptions. If one postulates monotheism as the only "true" and acceptable position, then one may be inclined to deny to the experience of communion with nature the ultimate achievement of a personal union with God. On the other hand, both the pantheist and the panentheist will arrive at a different conclusion, since both of them will view God as either identical with nature or, at any rate, as immanent in it. So it seems to me that this question must remain open to the various postulates that men make regarding the nature of the deity.

A similar problem arises in the fact of the "firm unanimous teaching of all the Catholic mystics and theologians alike, that contemplation, especially the higher mystical states, is supernatural in the strict sense of the word, the work of God Himself, the result of the indwelling of the Holy Ghost in the soul, and of the divine graces and gifts He bestows." [22] The problem here is different from the one discussed immediately above in that the argument hinges on the affirmation by mystics and theologians that the experiences are God-induced. As long as we remain at this level, Stace's principle of causal indifference is applicable. Abbot Butler's words to this point are but a reaffirmation of Stace's contention:

> The experiences of all the mystics, non-Christian as well as Christian, are couched in the same language;

all make, in one way or another, the same claim of entering into an immediate relation and contact with the Divinity or with Ultimate Reality. The resemblance, the identity, of the descriptions are unmistakable for anyone who will read the experiences on the one side and the other.[23]

A final objection must be met here. Some authors place the drug-induced experience on the same level as that of nature mystics, and thus distinguish it from the theistic experiences. This seems to be the basic position taken by R. C. Zaehner in his reply to Aldous Huxley's *The Doors of Perception,* and, it must be noted, after he himself experimented (unsuccessfully) with mescaline. Zaehner's argument, basically, distinguishes between the spontaneous or God-induced experiences and those induced by drugs or other less traditional means, and he credits only the former with genuineness.

But Zaehner's point is misleading. For, in the first place, there is no proper way to distinguish between the use of a drug in order to induce a mystical experience and the use of fasting, scourges, yoga, penances, prolonged meditation, whirling dances, and so forth, for the same purpose. The only differences might be speed and pleasantness. As Hoffer and Osmond remark:

So difficult has it been to achieve these states of mysticism that man has considered it almost immoral should they come with little effort. In fact, one of the greatest criticisms of the psychedelic experience is that it comes rather too easily, as if only what is attainable with extreme difficulty is valuable. The experience is debased, so they say, unless the price is high.[24]

This opinion they call "the immediate thoughtless re-action of the ignorant." This is precisely what is meant by Stace's causal *indifference*. As Spinks remarks:

> If drugs produce experiences which seem to be pseudo-transcendental in character then the experi-ences which follow the self-inflicted tortures of as-cetics, Christian and non-Christian alike, are by the same token, open to the same objection. There is psychologically and chemically very little difference between taking a drug and submitting oneself to such masochistic mortifications as those endured by the Blessed Suso, except that the former is pleasant and the latter horrifyingly painful. The nervous system is always being affected chemically. When the Lenten fast is observed with strictness for forty days, the chemistry of the body is strongly affected. Many of the most vivid visions of the medieval mystics seem to have occurred during periods of prolonged fasting. . . . On a purely chemical basis, it could be argued that mystical insights which appear to be associated with alterations of the chemistry of the body are not essentially different from the insights which it is claimed can be experienced by the administration of drugs.[25]

In short, there is no such thing as a *purely* religious ex-perience: they all are psychosomatic in one way or another. In the words of Huston Smith, "from the psychopharma-cological standpoint we now understand these states to be the products of changes in brain chemistry." [26] Further-more, as Timothy Leary remarks, the very same chemical processes released or activated by drugs may be more or less normal to some few people, who are thus "chemically" predisposed to mystical experiences.[27]

This leads us to another important point, namely, the

importance of personality and context in the religious experience. Experience is highly individualistic. "As a mind attuned to metaphysics has metaphysical intuitions, so will a mind attuned to religion have religious intuitions," said Abbot Butler.[28] Spinks remarks that "human beings interpret their experiences not only in terms of belief but also in terms of their own personality." [29] The La Guardia Report (1944) on the use of marijuana already stated that variances in effects were due to "differences in the mental makeup of the subjects, and the particular state of mind and responsiveness at the time." Moreover, as any drug user will attest, the receptiveness of the circumstances is very important, especially for a "good trip." This matter has been further confirmed in clinical research, and the terms "set" (the subject's expectations) and "setting" (the social and climacteric atmosphere) are used to express them. Hoffer and Osmond, for instance, describe under "set" the following factors: personality, somatotype education, vocation, age, health, reasons for taking drugs, prior experience with hallucinogens, previous psychiatric therapy, premedications, circadian rhythm, relation to meals. Under "setting," they list the therapist or friend (that is, his orientation, objectives, knowledge, trustworthiness), the physical environment, the number of people present, visual and auditory aids.[30]

Leary's research showed that

> a definite relationship existed between set, setting, and the type of result. Those subjects who approached the experience with hopeful, serious intentions and who sensed a supportive environment learned more and changed the most.[31]

Huston Smith asserts that

given the right set and setting, the drugs can induce religious experiences indistinguishable from experiences that occur spontaneously. Nor need set and setting be exceptional. The way statistics are currently running, it looks as if from one-fourth to one-third of the general population will have religious experiences if they take the drugs under naturalistic conditions, meaning by this conditions in which the researcher supports the subject but does not try to influence the direction his experience will take. Among subjects who have strong religious inclinations to begin with, the proportion of those having religious experiences jumps to three-fourths. If they take the drugs in settings that are religious too, the ratio soars to nine in ten.[32]

This is not surprising. Both factors have been known to play an important role in the history of mysticism. The seeker's character and intentions have been paramount, and even the environment has been of great importance. Witness the association of men in communities of like mind and purpose, with a distinctive "spirit," the solitary establishment of their monasteries, the beauty of the sites, often the most astonishing in the area, and the atmosphere of silence and recollection deliberately created as an aid to the experience.

I mentioned above that speed and pleasantness might be the only difference between a drug-induced and a conventionally induced religious experience. But this statement is liable to misinterpretation, and so I should say a word about the matter of quickness. Those who sing the glories of the drug experience and assimilate it to the mystical states are often accused of advocating "instant mysticism," "the semblance of enlightenment without benefit of discipline." [33] As far as I know, this accusation is unfounded.

As Leary himself has indicated, the drug experience requires discipline if wholesome results are to ensue and if these are to be enduring.[34] In any drug experience, and *a fortiori* in the therapeutic, the metaphysical, and the religious one, the trip guide plays a role second only to the tripster's character and the setting.[35] From the therapeutic point of view, this is obvious and needs no further elaboration. If the purpose of the trip is therapeutic, no one ought to take LSD except under the guidance and supervision of a competent psychiatrist or physician. From the metaphysical and religious point of view, the need for guidance is corroborated by the ages-long history of religious advisers, persons of integral character who had already walked up the paths of mysticism and were then ready to lead others in their own pursuit of enlightenment. One of the most convincing statements of the need for expert guidance is that of Carlos Castaneda, *The Teachings of Don Juán: A Yaqui Way of Knowledge*,[36] but similar accounts abound in the various religious traditions of East and West.

From all that has preceded, it becomes clear, I think, that drug-induced experiences as well as traditionally labeled metaphysical or religious experiences obtained through contemplation or other means can properly be called identical as far as their phenomenological content is concerned. Of course, I am not so naïve as to maintain that the first intake of LSD will send the young person into ecstasy and the vision of God, but neither would I maintain that the first effort in monastic contemplation results always in magnificent metaphysical or religious insights.

Obviously, many people use drugs, yet their experiences remain fairly pedestrian; and many people have gone, and continue to go into monasteries, yet remain unenlightened. In both instances, however, in the case of the young tripster and in that of the monastic tyro, the impetus, the underlying reason for their diverse activities (in a city alley or in an abbey cell), is the search for some insight into the meaning of it all, the urge for at least a momentary escape from the prison of the ordinary, long enough to catch a glimpse and be refreshed by the beauty, peace, cohesiveness, of the nonordinary. From this point of view, both types of activity are symptomatic of deep underlying concerns. Neither experience should be downgraded or rejected *a priori*. "God is not tied down to any sacrament," runs the old Scholastic adage. For many, the LSD cube may be the beginning sacramental initiation into a world hitherto closed.[37] But initiation does not mean fullness or completion.

Traditionally, in all cultures, though often by varied names, the *way* of religious experience has been divided into three stages: the *purgative,* where there occurs a reevaluation of earthly views and possessions; the *illuminative,* where further understanding and peace are attained; and the *unitive,* where one is more aware of the presence of God and feels united to him. There is no time rule for any of these. In ages past, men spent years striving to extricate themselves from particular views of the world. But some achieved a "conversion" almost instantly. The use of drugs may be a particularly effective way of achieving the unmasking of the self and of reality needed to become aware of the nonordinary dimensions of human existence,[38] it may mark the start of a revolt against the pursuit of ultimate objectivity,[39] it may help the user to realize, or begin to realize, that "the entire man, who feels all needs by turns, will take nothing as an equivalent for life but the fulness of living itself." [40] The evidence to date suggests that in proper circumstances (= setting), and in certain people properly disposed (= set), the psychotropic drugs have a strong tendency to initiate genuine religious experience.[41]

But the question of the genuineness of the experience still bothers us, and it must be settled if the argument is to prove fully convincing. When doubts about the genuineness of any transcendental experience—artistic, metaphysical, or religious—continue to be felt, there is one final criterion that can be applied, one that cannot be doubted, and beyond which there is no recourse, namely, *change of character*. Undoubtedly, this criterion is somewhat external to the experiences themselves, but in many respects it is intimately connected with them. "You will recognize them by the fruits they bear" (Matt. 7:16). Such has been the case with traditional religious experience, for the mystics "were what they were, not in spite of their mysticism, but because of it." [42] This is so also in the case of drug-induced experiences. In the many interviews with young people that preceded the writing of this book one thing was clear beyond the shadow of a doubt: *all* of them affirmed that their experiences had changed their lives for the better.[43] In such instances it is no longer permissible to deny the genuineness of the experience. As William James argues:

The unseen region in question is not merely ideal, for it produces effects in this world. When we commune with it, work is actually done upon our finite personality, for we are turned into new men, and consequences in the way of conduct follow in the natural world upon our regenerative change. But that which produces effects within another reality must be termed a reality itself.[44]

This criterion, therefore, applies to both the drug-induced and the ascetically induced or otherwise contrived religious experience. I am saying, briefly, that it is not "how" the experience is induced that constitutes a criterion of its genuineness, nor only "what" is experienced during the trance—for phenomenological descriptions, as I have indicated, are identical, and as mystics and spiritual directors know only too well, deception is easy to come by—but the way in which a man's life is changed as a result of the experience.[45] In the words of Aldous Huxley:

> Psychic experiences which do not contribute to sanctification are not experiences of God but merely of certain unfamiliar aspects of our psychophysical universe. . . . Where there is no evidence of sanctification, there is no reason to suppose that the experience has anything to do with God.[46]

That this is, or is not, always the case, cannot be assumed *a priori* with regard to any mystical experience, no matter how induced. To quote James once more:

> Our spiritual judgment, . . . our opinion of the significance and value of a human event or condition, must be decided on empirical grounds exclusively. If the *fruits for life* of the state of conversion are good, we ought to idealize and venerate it, even though it be a piece of natural psychology; if not, we ought to make short work with it, no matter what supernatural being may have infused it.[47]

As I have said, I have come across young men for whom the drug experience, with obvious religious overtones, was the beginning of "conversion," a change of life still enduring after several years. But I do not imply that this is the general rule. However, the strength of the arguments presented suggests that enlightenment is generally the intent whenever psychotropic drugs are used seriously. This implies that an amelioration of one's life, an increase in joyful expectations, is generally a causative element of the drug experience. These last two statements are but explications of the claim I have been trying to substantiate, namely, that drug use is symptomatic of an underlying religious concern. Furthermore, I have maintained that consciously or unconsciously the drug user and the religious tyro express in varied ways the same concern for ultimate reality whose proof is the changed life.

A final point must be added here with regard to change of life as a criterion. One reason why such a behavioral criterion is of the utmost importance is the very serious danger of quietism, the temptation of passivity in the expectation of visions, leading to the temptation to be so enthralled by the expanding awareness of beauty in nonordinary reality that one does nothing to beautify this very ordinary reality of day-to-day living. The temptation is even greater when the drug-induced experience is, at the same time, a relief from a harrowing home atmosphere or other similarly tortuous circumstance. Sidney Jourard expresses this point as follows:

Growing experience and the experience of growth has another dimension besides increased receptivity to the disclosures of the world. I refer here to the activation of experiential modes and qualities that ordinarily are repressed or limited, in the service of one's projects. If one is at work on a job, or seeking to convince someone of something, he remembers and represses his recall in those ways that serve the project; he imagines and represses imagination in ways that serve the project; he reasons and conceptualizes in

ways that serve the project. He even feels and represses feeling in service of the project. Drop projects, as happens with drug use, or with dropping out,
or on Sunday, and the modes and qualities become
activated, enriching one's experience of being incredi-
bly. If a person's capacities to imagine, think and
reason, recall, fantasy and will are activated more
fully, he will have started a growth cycle. But new
perceptions, memories, fantasies do not yield growth
unless a person incorporates these into expanded concepts. This he will do—he will restabilize his world—
*only if he forms new projects for the future as com-
pelling as those he has abandoned.*[48]

Already in Plato we find a warning against idle contemplation. The seers who, after a laborious search—a
"steep and rugged ascent" [49]—have attained the vision of
Goodness, "must not be allowed, as they now are, to remain in the heights, refusing to come down again to the
prisoners [in the Cave] or to take any part in their la-
bours." [50] Paul asks his Christians to "keep away from
any brother who is living in idleness" (II Thess. 3:6), and
even gives them this command: "If any one will not work,
let him not eat" (v. 10). Augustine warns of too much
readiness to find delight in idle vacancy,[51] and in the Zen
tradition Hyakujo's "No work, no eating" simply dupli-
cates Paul's injunction.[52] When such advice is not heeded,
tripping, no matter how induced, becomes a true "opium
of the people" (in Marx's celebrated phrase), for it re-
duces man to inertia and prevents him from engaging in
the constructive work needed all around him. If anything,
the reality revealed to him in his vision ought to be a blue-
print for action, not the enticement to self-complacent in-
activity.

2. The Human Need for Religious Experience

So far, I have only established the sameness of the drug-induced experience and the traditional religious experience, depending on their actually meeting certain criteria, especially that of a changed life. The claim, however, that I have made, that the very fact of drug use is symptomatic of ultimate concerns, does not rest only on the identity of the experiences. The causal link, as I have observed above, goes beyond, to a basic human need.[53] There are at least two ways of representing this human need. The first has recourse to a theory of instincts and their corresponding emotions. The second arises out of the consideration of man's inner development, as he ventures through the crisis of identity. Both ways, really, say the same thing, but they express it in a different manner. I will deal first with the theory that sees man's needs for consciousness expansion as arising from instinct.

The human need I have in mind may be termed the *instinct of completeness*.[54] By terming it instinct I imply, of course, that I am talking about a rigidly patterned mechanism of responses, not learned, and found in all members of the same species.[55] Various psychologists identify this particular instinct with curiosity, or with orientation, or with self-assertion. The terms are immaterial for my purposes here. I am talking about an observable instinct or innate mechanism that seeks completeness whenever it is confronted with a sense or awareness of incompleteness, of limitations, of gaps in the situation encountered. Fromm calls it "the need for a frame of orientation and an object of devotion," and he maintains that the thesis that this instinct "is rooted in the conditions of man's existence seems to be amply verified by the fact of the universal occurrence of religion in history." [56] Elsewhere Fromm explains it as follows:

> The disharmony of man's existence generates needs which far transcend those of his natural origins. These needs result in an imperative drive to restore a unity and equilibrium between himself and the rest of nature. He makes the attempt to restore this unity and equilibrium in the first place in thought by constructing an all-inclusive mental picture of the world which serves as a frame of reference from which he can derive an answer to the question of where he stands and what he ought to do. But such thought-systems are not sufficient. . . . He has to strive for the experience of unity and oneness in all spheres of his being in order to find a new equilibrium. Hence any satisfying system of orientation implies not only intellectual elements but elements of feeling and sense to be realised in action in all fields of human endeavor. Devotion to an aim, or an idea, or a power transcending man such as God, is an expression of this need for completeness in the process of living. [57]

For Camus, it is precisely this nostalgia for unity and completeness, this appetite for the absolute, this insistence upon being "at-oned" with the universe, that illustrates the essential impulse of the human drama. [58]

Now the religious experience characteristically assuages this thirst in the fullest sense. By its all-inclusiveness, by its involvement of the nonrational, by its general quality of reverence, it is the only human experience that can fully correspond to this human need. [59] The connection of the instinct for completeness and the emotion or sense of reverence (characteristic of the religious experience) that satisfies it is predicated in terms of McDougall's "hormic" interpretation of instincts,[60] according to which man has instincts or propensities that, when activated, become associated with an affective quality which we call emotion. This connection is of great importance for the substantiation of my claim that drug use is symptomatic of an underlying concern. The characteristics of the religious experience described above are, in fact, emotional in character. The sameness of the religious experience, whether induced by drugs or by other means, implies, therefore, a sameness in emotional content, even though there may be great differences in the degrees of intensity of these emotions, and in their various combinations and emphases. All this establishes these experiences as *the* symptom or behavioral manifestation of the activated instinct for completeness. The fact of the natural connection between instinct and emotion, as explained above, is the causal link that completes the chain I have been trying to validate.

The second way of establishing a natural causal connection between ultimate concerns and a basic human need is provided in the psychology of Erik Erikson as developed in his various works. I refer here primarily to Erikson's fifth stage in man's development, the crisis of identity versus role confusion characteristic of puberty and adolescence. The beginning of youth is marked by a crisis wherein the former continuities established earlier are questioned once more, and a search for "a new sense of continuity and sameness" takes place. As Erikson explains it:

> The integration now taking place in the form of ego identity is . . . more than the sum of the childhood identifications. It is the accrued experiences of the ego's ability to integrate all identifications with the vicissitudes of the libido, with the aptitudes developed

out of endowment, and with the opportunities offered in social roles. The sense of ego identity, then, is the accrued confidence that the inner sameness and continuity prepared in the past are matched by the sameness and continuity of one's meaning for others.[61]

This identity crisis, Erikson continues,

occurs in that period of the life cycle when each youth must forge for himself some central perspective and direction, some working unity, out of the effective remnants of his childhood and the hopes of his anticipated adulthood; he must detect some meaningful resemblance between what he has come to see in himself and what his sharpened awareness tells him others judge and expect him to be.[62]

It should be noted that this crisis is not purely a matter of personal individual growth. As Erikson stresses, "we cannot separate personal growth and communal change"; much less can we separate "the identity crisis in individual life and contemporary crises in historical development because the two help to define each other and are truly relative to each other." [63]

Now, young people today are not at all immune to this maturational crisis. Like adolescents of all times and places, they are going through a phase of development whose successful resolution is necessary for further maturation and final integrity.[64] But just as at certain times and in some people this identity crisis will be minimal, in other people at other times this crisis will be truly revolutionary, a second birth, marked by social turbulence, delinquent behavior, and by passionate involvement in causes.[65] To say simply that youth today are in the midst of an extraordinary identity crisis is an obvious understatement. Still the reasons for this upheaval must be explored, even though in brief fashion.

One of the primary characteristics of the adolescent as he passes—in James's fine phrase—"from the child's small universe to the wide intellectual and spiritual life of maturity" [66] is the need for an ideology within whose folds he will be able to define himself. This ideology may be highly structured and routinized, like the military, political, and religious "societies" that have existed in all civilizations. On the other hand, it may be a way of life, a *Weltanschauung*—in Erikson's words, "an utopian outlook, a cosmic mood, or a doctrinal logic, all shared as self-evident beyond any need for demonstration." [67] Now, as studies of drug use among youth have shown, the creation of such outlooks is one of the striking effects of hallucinogenic experiences.

But together with the need for this universal outlook is a need to reject and repudiate the consciousness of the past as insufficient and even inimical to one's own self-determination. The identity crisis transpires within a dialectic of negation of whatever is limiting and destructive in one's past, individual and social, and an affirmation of emerging awarenesses, again both individual and social.[68]

In the identity crisis the adolescent revolts against the limits imposed on his humanity and simultaneously reaches out toward the expanding vistas of human potentiality. In Camus's sense, the adolescent is a rebel, that is, a man who says no, but whose refusal *ipso facto* entails the affirmation of something whose betrayal one will not tolerate.[69]

Today the adolescent experiences an all-out assault upon his newly emerging self. His need for privacy, liberty, self-respect, is thwarted at every step, especially by the schools in which he finds himself incarcerated, and in the home, where parents do not realize that the world, like them-

selves, is changing.[70] Today, in our society, as an individual reaches adolescence he finds it increasingly difficult
—nay, and ever more suicidal—to identify himself even
partially with the social web woven all around him by his
elders. So he revolts. As Sidney Jourard puts it,

> When they smoke marijuana and take LSD, I believe
> young people are declaring how they find prescribed
> life in this society, how they view their elders—us—
> our values, our way of life, the role models we are.
> They are saying they don't like it.[71]

The adolescent's rejection of his parents' world is the
rejection also of an ideology that supports that world, an
ideology with which he cannot identify, within which he
cannot affirm himself. It is the rejection of a narrow outlook, a world closed in upon itself. It is the rejection of
conditions that repress expanding consciousness; it is, in
Charles Reich's terms, the rejection of Consciousness II
and, simultaneously, the affirmation of Consciousness III.
This rejection is not the adolescent's fault but the fault of
the society that nurtured him. Whenever a society offers its
youth the technological, economic, ideological, and human
conditions within which youthful vitality can discern the
promise of a future, the identity crisis is transcended in
an affirmative and exciting way. However, as Erikson remarks:

> Where this is not given, the adolescent mind becomes
> a more explicitly ideological one, by which we mean
> one searching for some inspiring unification of tradi-
> tion or anticipated techniques, ideas, and ideals. And,
> indeed, it is the ideological potential of a society
> which speaks most clearly to the adolescent who is
> so eager to be affirmed by peers, to be confirmed by

teachers, and to be inspired by worthwhile "ways of life." On the other hand, should a young person feel that the environment tries to deprive him too radically of all the forms of expression which permit him to develop and integrate the next step, he may resist with the wild strength encountered in animals who are suddenly forced to defend their lives. For, indeed, in the social jungle of human existence, there is no feeling of being alive without a sense of identity.[72]

One cannot live without a sense of identity. In a world which increasingly looks as if it were headed up a blind alley, and in which increasingly one senses worry, fear, and despair, there are only two ways for one to react: passionate commitment, or abandonment.[73] In James's words, one way is "that an opposite affection should overpoweringly break over us, and the other is by getting so exhausted with the struggle that we have to stop—so we drop down, give up, and *don't care* any longer." [74] Both attitudes are present in our world today. The important thing to note here, once more, is that both originate in the natural, inevitable effort to find oneself, to gain the sense of one's own identity. Against a backdrop on which is writ large NO EXIT, the drug-using adolescent is earnestly expressing "the simple and fervent wish for a hallucinatory sense of unity." [75] Thus the need for consciousness expansion is, again, established, and it becomes possible to see the interlocking of the chain I am trying to validate.

3. A HUMAN NEED THWARTED

In the growing literature on the drug subculture perhaps the most engrossing and captivating narratives are the first-person accounts of parents whose children are suddenly discovered to be drug users. The accounts are poignant and pathetic. They bespeak of tragedy in a very real sense of an irrevocable and unrelenting fate driving each participant toward an ineluctable and painful end. The cry that often rises to the parents' lips is almost typical of the bewilderment of "the generation over thirty": "Where have we failed our children?" The immediate impression is that of sincere men and women intent on providing for their children whatever was best in all respects, who suddenly wonder what else they could have provided in order to avert the dread event. The notion is that something has gone wrong somewhere, that something needed was not at hand, and that this lack entails a failure on the part of the provider.

It seems to me that this remorseful cry entails a deeper sense of failure than that of not having provided for what was needed. Today, many of my generation wonder aloud and ask, How could we have made the mistake of producing youth who take with such desperate seriousness what we have studiously striven to ignore? For as a society we have determinedly tried to suppress all concern for ultimate realities, all interest in values that cannot be measured in terms of military victory, industrial productivity, business success, social acceptability, scientific objectivity, money, and legality. Yet our youth are subordinating all these palpable achievements to the idealism of an ultimate experience, and they are doing so precisely with the help of drugs. As Roszak writes:

> If one starts with a sense of the person that ventures to psychoanalytical depths, one may rapidly arrive at a viewpoint that rejects many of the hitherto undisputed values of industrialism itself. One soon begins talking about "standards of living" that transcend high productivity, efficiency, full employment, and the work-and-consumption ethic. Quality and not quantity becomes the touchstone of social value.[76]

But there is still a further sense of the cry, subtler and in a way more pathetic. The "Where have we failed our children?" is really a euphemism for the more anguished self-pitying "Where have we failed ourselves?" We seem, in fact, to be saying that perhaps we have done something wrong to ourselves. I am sure that not too many of the anxious generation over thirty admit this, or are conscious of it—after all, we do have compensatory mechanisms to color our decisions in the most rosy shades. Yet herein lies the worst aspect of the tragedy. For an awareness of the failure might intimate a beginning of regeneration; but an ignorance of it and, worse still, an inability to admit even the possibility of one's being wrong do not augur very well for the future. My task here, therefore, consists in pointing to where *we* have gone wrong with regard to our children and to ourselves. Many books have appeared over the past decade or so that have attempted similar tasks. My concern is somewhat narrower in scope, since I want to delineate only our failures vis-à-vis the particular human need for completeness, for *Weltanschauung*.

There are mainly five factors I consider to be primarily responsible for the thwarting of man's desire for wholeness. I call them *Idols,* for they are the gods of our times. It is interesting to note that our society, which claims enlightenment from myth, is as mythological as any that preceded it.

The essence of idolatry is the worship of that which man has made. "Idolatry," writes Fromm, "is always the worship of something into which man has put his own creative powers, and to which he now submits." [77] Our Idols are *Idol of Science, Idol of Objectivity, Idol of the Church, Idol of the Secular, Idol of Neutrality.* I would like to say a few words about each of them.

The *Idol of Science* is a monster. Its tentacles are ubiquitous, its power is "know-how," its kingdom is technocracy, its parent is reason, its children are industry, business, war. All modern men sacrifice at its altar, for such sacrifices bring the blessing of comfort. To this Idol we bring dignity, freedom, interest, excitement, sexuality, morality, even life itself. This Idol devours everything, and what it rejects carries upon its forehead the stigma of damnation: in our society the worst fate for man or idea is to be branded "unscientific." The religious experience has been so named, and has therefore been relegated to the outskirts of town, where the sickened and outcasts must make their dwelling. To this Idol we have dedicated our own children, who are known as "children of the atomic age," "children of the industrial revolution," "children of science and progress."

The *Idol of Objectivity* is Science's brother. It dictates the extent of our interest, the "thing" or object to which one must attach oneself, the "number" to which one must be betrothed, the "quantity" by which one must be ruled. This is the Idol of "having," not of "being," for who can measure being? This Idol has decreed that there is "nothing" in a religious experience, since it is purely subjective, since it cannot be numbered, measured, quantified. Mysticism is either the result of sickened livers and overworked brains, or else meaningless illusion. Whoever makes a claim to such mystical insights must endure the anathema of subjectivism.

The *Idol of the Church* is Kafka's Castle, the prison that holds and kills imperceptibly, but against which it is sinful to revolt. It is the Grand Inquisitor, organizing human freedom until the spirit flees the man, and he performs, worships, pays tithes, kisses the ring, like an automaton. The Idol of the Church arises because of a fatal "conversion" that turns a means into an end, and from protector of the religious it turns to persecutor and despiser.

This Idol and the worship it commands deserve a few words of further clarification, since it is somewhat easier to discover idolatries in a secular context than it is to distinguish them from the true worship in a sacred context. However, much has been written about "the failure of the churches," and my concern here is therefore restricted to one particular aspect of this failure.

In his book *Honest to God,* Bishop Robinson states a principle that is fundamentally applicable in the present context. He makes the point that human beings seem always to find it necessary to set up images and myths to rivet, as it were, their attention while they endeavor to hold converse with the Other. Structures are also set up designed to preserve the images, to perpetuate them, to help the young understand the original meanings, to expound these meanings and understandings to others, and so forth. It is but natural that men do so, given their nature and their tendency to anthropomorphism. But, adds

Robinson—and this is the main point I have in mind—
"as soon as they [the images and structures] become a
substitute for God, as soon as they *become* God, *so that
what is not embodied in the image is excluded or denied,*
then we have a new idolatry." [78] In other words, when the
structure, which is supposed to be a means to an end, becomes the end, we have a "conversion." When the church,
which is supposed to be a means to the experience of God
by man becomes itself the goal that man must meet and
experience, we have idolatry.

That this has unfortunately taken place is unquestion-
able, even though the degree to which it has in the many
denominations and sects varies considerably. Evidence of
this happening is plentiful and multifaceted. The result is
always the same: the human need for a meaningful experience is thwarted, for the emphasis is on the rituals,
the performances, the dogmas, the knowledge particular
to each denomination. As Dewey stated it:

> The present depression in religion is closely con-
> nected with the fact that religions now prevent, be-
> cause of their weight of historic encumbrances, the
> religious quality of experience from coming to con-
> sciousness and finding the expression that is appro-
> priate to present conditions, intellectual and moral. I
> believe that such is the case. I believe that many per-
> sons are so repelled from what exists as a religion
> by its intellectual and moral implications, that they
> are not even aware of attitudes in themselves that if
> they came to fruition would be genuinely religious.[79]

Professor Karl Rahner, one of the most noted theologians of our time, has expressed very clearly this idolatry
which I am trying to expound. He writes: "In Your book
it is written of You, O God, that You are Spirit, and Your

Holy Spirit is called the Spirit of Freedom: 'The Lord is Spirit; and where the Spirit of the Lord is, there is freedom' (2 Cor. 3:17). . . . But," he goes on,

> You have established rulers in this world, both temporal and spiritual, and sometimes it seems to me that they have diligently set about patching up all the holes that Your Spirit of freedom had torn in the fence of rules and regulations by His liberating Pentecostal storm.
>
> First there are the 2414 paragraphs of the Church's lawbook. And even these haven't sufficed: how many *"responsa"* to inquiries have been added to bring joy to the hearts of the jurists! And then there are several thousand liturgical decrees clamoring for our attention. In order to praise You in the Breviary "in psalms and hymns and spiritual songs," in order to "sing and make melody in the heart" (Eph. 5:19), I need a road map, a *directorium,* so intricate and elaborate that it requires a new edition every year.
>
> Then there are also the various "official bulletins" in the Kingdom of Your Holy Spirit, not to mention countless files, inquiries, replies, reports, decisions, meetings, citations, instructions from every kind of Congregation and Commission. And how resourceful the moralists are at asking tricky questions, until all the pronouncements of all higher authorities are neatly ordered and interpreted.
>
> And what delicate calculations must go into the granting of an indulgence! Only recently some learned theologians found occasion to dispute whether a sick person is obliged to kiss the crucifix of Your Son fourteen times, or six times, or less, in order to gain an indulgence. What incredible zeal Your servants and stewards have shown in Your absence, during the long period while You have been away on Your

journey into the distant silence of eternity! And yet, according to Your own word, where the Spirit of the Lord is, there is freedom! [80]

The structures that Rahner is questioning, that over-abundance of the letter of the law which kills the spirit, is precisely what the Grand Inquisitor, that arch-representative of the churches, refers to when he tells the Prisoner about the freedom he promised men nineteen hundred years ago.

"Did You not often say then, 'I will make you free'? But now You have seen these 'free' men," the old man adds suddenly, with a pensive smile. "Yes, we've paid dearly for it," he goes on, looking sternly at Him, "but at last we have completed that work in Your name. For fifteen centuries we have been wrestling with Your freedom, but now it is ended and over for good. . . . Now, today, people are more persuaded than ever that they are completely free, yet they have brought their freedom to us and laid it humbly at our feet. But that has been our doing." [81]

How well has organized religion achieved this purpose of wresting to itself the worship due to God by emphasizing the structure and the law, and by suspicioning and excluding the freedom of the religious experience, is amply apparent in the millions of automated worshipers who crowd our temples Sunday after Sunday, in the strictures hurled at those who seek freedom and communion of worship,[82] in the suspicion that has been cast upon religious experience especially since the Renaissance, and in the stigma still attached to mysticism, no matter how induced, by the ecclesiastical powers that be.[83] Saint Teresa of Ávila relates of herself how her spiritual experiences became suspect to the extent that she was investigated by a number of theologians. Their unanimous conclusion was that she was being deceived by the Devil.[84] It did not occur to the learned men that their conclusion was, itself, idolatrous.

The *Idol of the Secular* is a wine that has gone sour. For it surely is a boon to man to find space within his daily comings and goings where he can tread without fear of a booming voice that warns, "Tread softly, this is holy ground!" To demythologize, to limit the tendency of the sacred to encroach on the secular, this is good. But to desacralize the universe in such a way that man is no longer able to find infinite depths of meaning in the simple tasks and events of life, this is not good. And the situation is not devoid of irony, for the claim of the Secular for the exclusivity of human concern is but an effort to establish a self-idolatrous worship.

I should explain this further. Demythologization does not necessarily lead to desacralization. It is one thing to separate the domains of the sacred and the profane; it is quite another to refuse or be unable to see infinite depths of meaning in things, events, and experiences labeled profane. The first separation between the sacred and the profane occurs on a horizontal level, as it were. The latter is a matter of vertical penetration. The fact that Teilhard de Chardin could distinguish between his strictly religious duties and his archaeological work did not entail for him the refusal or inability to see in the latter a manifestation of the Spirit. "A religious perspective on anything at all results from seeing the meaning of it in relation to the supreme object of one's commitment," writes Phenix.[85] Yet nothing at all is lost of the secular reality of the objects or events thus perceived.[86] The object remains what it is in itself within its environment. But for those who can

see, the object becomes an epiphany of limitless possibilities—in fact, a hierophany. It is this possibility which
is proscribed in the worship of Secularism.

Finally, we come to the *Idol of Neutrality,* the multi-
farious worship of what cannot truly be, yet which draws
multitudes in its wake because of its apparent respectabil-
ity. It is the wolf in sheep's skin. One of its pelts is the
constitutional separation between church and state. This
separation, about which there have been endless controversies, obscures the main point, namely, that the so-called
neutrality of our institutions is an impossible chimera, and
that there is more to religion than the ecclesiastical institutions.

If one accepts the horizontal distinction between the
sacred and the secular, there is little doubt, it seems to me,
that it is proper and advantageous for society to have a
separation between those institutions devoted to religion,
that is, to the sacred, and those concerned with the man-
agement of the secular. It is silly, even, to contend that
such a separation is antireligion. From the simple admin-
istrative point of view, it is expedient to have different
institutions handle different human concerns without en-
croaching on each other. But this is far removed from the
claim that this separation *ipso facto* creates a neutral state.
Many have wanted to believe so, and in their blind eager-
ness have created for themselves an Idol whose existence
they zealously guard. Theoretically, maybe, and in the abstract, by neither fostering nor hindering religion, the state
is neutral. But in fact, it cannot be. For institutions are
peopled, and people are not neutral.

This is clearly demonstrated by the Supreme Court's
decision barring prayers in the public schools. The public
school, the argument runs, insofar as it forms part of the

state, must not be associated with any specific religion, not even with religion as opposed to nonreligion. The public school must be neutral. But the Supreme Court's decision has *not,* in fact, established any neutrality. From the *purely* theoretical and constitutional point of view, neutrality in the public schools (with respect to religion) would entail allowing children and teachers to pray if they wished to, to teach and learn religion if they wished to, not to pray and not to learn about religion if they didn't want to, and to be, in fact, both pro and anti religion if they wished to, all this at the same time and with the same degree of freedom. But this is clearly not the case. The goal of neutrality, its aim and perfection, is truth, both in thinking and in practice. True neutrality would logically and justly demand the equal acceptance of all religions, nonreligion, and antireligion, both as views and as practices, within the school situation. But we are far from the realization of such *pure* neutrality.

For centuries now, and especially after the Civil War, the Idol of Neutrality has wrought havoc on the lives of our children. The disestablishment clause, meant to apply to institutions, has led to practices in our schools that have conveyed to our children *one* message, namely, that nonreligion is the modern, scientific, American attitude. I am not saying that this has been officially proclaimed as the aim of the schools, but that the impression created has been one, not of neutrality, but of nonreligion. "The medium is the message," and the medium has been one, not of neutrality, but of nonreligion. The message has been correspondingly picked up loud and clear—until the youth of today protest.

Why this is so can be explained in various ways. My own explanation is framed in terms of the assumption, stated above, that the goal of neutrality is truth both in thought and in practice. In the context of the present discussion I maintained earlier that men naturally seek after holistic experiences that may give meaning and consistence to all their other experiences. The truth of man, therefore, in this context is his search for meaning. Ideally, in a pure and abstract sense, neutrality would allow every man to search and find his truth. But once the truth is found, neutrality ceases, for its goal is truth. And if the truth has been found and established beforehand, there can be no room for neutrality, for the same reason. Men are not neutral toward the bubonic plague or toward cancer. If neutrality continues, it does so at the expense of man's truth—and in that case it can hardly be called neutrality. In the face of man's truth pure neutrality, as we have described it, ends up being for evil. In other words, once the truth is found, partisanship is the only possible course —partisanship, that is, in the furtherance of the human truth. If the truth found is not final, one can keep an open mind, one can continue to search, one can seek refinement, but one cannot be neutral.

Pure neutrality does not allow equally every individual child to find out for himself what the truth of man is. For, in fact, it does not allow him to be religious. The proof of this is the existence of a separate system of religious education. But my argument against neutrality is even stronger. For if it is true, as I have maintained, that the truth of man involves his pursuit of ultimate meaning, then to claim and seek to establish neutrality in the face of this truth is to set oneself against this truth by allowing untruth an equal representation. This, in fact, is a denial of human perfection and self-realization. In the face of the truth of man's concerns, only a partisan cultivation of this truth is justifiable for the good of man.[87]

Aside from the question of neutrality, the infatuation with the principle of separation of the institutions of church and state has led us to consider the problem of religion in life purely from an institutional point of view. We have pitted *the institution of religion* against *the institution of the state,* but there is more to religion and to the state than is dreamed of in their institutions. Here, of course, I speak primarily about the religious *experience.* This has been the aspect neglected all along in the disputes and controversies regarding the separation between church and state. Because of the concern with the institutional aspects of religion, the emphasis has been on the dogma, on the theology, on the structure, on the rules. The very rich mystical tradition existing in the West has been all but forgotten even by the religious institutions themselves, to the extent that our young, when growing up in our culture, have felt compelled to go to the East for symbols and explanations which, in fact, are not at all lacking in the West.

As a culture, then, as a society, we have lost the ability to see the world in any but scientific, objective, secular, institutional terms.[88] I say *lost* because from the vantage point of historical perspective we know we once had this ability, but it has been repressed in us, in part, by the social idolatries I have just enumerated.[89] We have, even unaware, perpetrated upon ourselves "a grand reductive process," [90] making ourselves fit the technocracy we have created, rather than making the technocracy subservient to us. In Charles Reich's words, ours has been an "impoverishment by substitution." [91] The question to be confronted now is whether or not this failure can be corrected, for the very upsurge of our youth and their concern with drugs is a consequence of this failure.

CHAPTER 3

Programmatic Pointers: The Schools

I will be thy guide, and will lead thee hence through the eternal place.

—Dante, *Divine Comedy,* "Inferno," Canto I

Zzyr awoke from a fitful sleep. He had a dream that troubled him deeply. He dreamed that on a relatively ordinary day he was going about his usual business—mending gravity machines. While in the discharge of his duties, another's thoughts began to focus and reveal themselves in Zzyr's mind. In itself this was not at all unusual, since all, or supposedly all, of Woff's people possessed the power to project their thoughts and receive the thoughts of others. What disturbed Zzyr was the message he was receiving. Although all of Woff's people were supposed to use their faculties for the good of the race and not for individual gain, someone was perverting his extra sense. He was attempting to control other people's thoughts, and such an action could be a real threat.

Once all of Woff's people had developed their extra sense, it had been deemed unethical to try to influence another's thoughts so as to gain personal power. Thought projection had become a part of life, a tool for communication, and not a weapon or lever for personal aggrandizement. Understandably Zzyr was bewildered at first; he then became fearful. Although one person could not destroy what all of Woff's people had attained, the notion of personal power via thought control could easily spread and threaten the whole society.

Mmv was the town idiot. For some unknown reason he had never developed the ability to read or project thoughts, and he was therefore pitied. He could reason fairly well with his other senses, and therefore was not scorned by his more fortunate brothers. When Zzyr's anxiety became public knowledge (as most things quickly became when one thought about them too much), people began to behave oddly. Not aware of society's new trouble, Mmv questioned a passerby about the cause of his trouble and those of other passersby. The solution to the problem seemed amazingly simple to Mmv. If Woff's people could rid themselves of this extra sense, then no one could control it. The passerby relayed the information, and soon everyone was "tuning out," and speech was again being used for communication. Telephone service was resumed in order to facilitate long-distance communication, and anyone found using the now forbidden extra sense was quickly prosecuted and condemned.

It was of course necessary to retain a few talented people, permit them the use of what was forbidden, since someone was needed to check or censor the use of the extra sense. When violators of the law were caught, new institutions had to be devised. Aside from penal colonies, schools were established, and the young were instructed in how to sense properly.

A simple problem had spread rapidly. Not because many people had tried to use the extra sense for personal power, but because the society's anxiety over the sense suddenly gave rise to new temptations and created unwieldy fears. But the more restrictions placed upon the use of the extra sense, the more violators there were. The tragedy of Woff's people would not have been so great had they not begun to feel guilty about their extra sense. They were forced to deny a part of their experience of themselves, something that really was theirs, that was natural to them.

Zzyr awoke from his dream and thought of what might have happened had the dream been true. He decided that the people in his dream had foolishly tried to solve a problem by wiping it out of existence. They really had tried to save the toenail of society by amputating its foot. Would it not have been better to consider the problem and unify against the deviate? Maybe it would have been better for people to learn more about the various uses of their extra sense? Or perhaps Woff's people were stronger than he thought and could resist any deviate's mental exertions? Zzyr was unable to satisfy himself totally with an answer to his predicament. The misuse of the sense was frightening—the prevention of such misuse was doubtful, and the corruption of society was a serious possibility. After his dream Zzyr always had some trouble sleeping.[1]

The problem with this fiction is that it is not fictitious enough. From his earliest beginnings, man has been endowed with the ability to discover infinite depths of mean-

ing amid the various events that crowd into his daily rou-
tines. As far back into the past as we can see, we find man
wondering about nonordinary reality and employing a
variety of means to get behind ordinary appearances. Some
of these means have led to unwholesome consequences, and
their use has been fraught with danger. To be possessed
by the fullness of reality has always entailed risk—"No
one shall see God and live!"—and the very experience of
the plenitude of reality has imposed among men obligations
of no small weight. "Woe to me if I do not preach!" ex-
claimed the enlightened Paul (I Cor. 9:16), and Socrates
asked the jury that was to deliberate on his fate whether
it was more proper to please men or to heed the promptings
of inspiration.[2] Both men died in the pursuit of the awareness they had attained.

Most societies have been wary of the visionary. We have
a long record of disinheriting enlightened ones, of banish-
ing and killing prophets, of casting suspicion on contempla-
tives, and of feeling terribly threatened by those who "see."
I think it is Leonardo da Vinci who says in his *Notebooks*
that the world's people fall neatly into three categories:
those who see, those who see when they are shown, and
those who do not see. We feel ill at ease in the company
of the seer. The taboo against seeing beyond the veil of
ordinary appearances has been a strong one indeed. We
seem to resent being found out, being truly exposed. In our
times, technocracy seems determined to prevent its being
proved a sham. The idolatries it has contrived to establish are a gigantic cover-up and a guarantee that the truth
will never be found.

But we may not have reckoned with the indomitable
spirit of man, the concrete man who strives to assert his
natural rights. As we successively endeavored to close

the various avenues to the beyond of nonordinary reality, man's ingenuity has come up with new ones, or has rediscovered old ones, or has reactivated unused ones. To be sure, some of these avenues are dangerous to travel. One needs guidance in *all* of them, and even then it is not possible to avoid all bad trips.[3] The point I am trying to make is that such unpleasant incidents are attendant upon the use of any and all means of achieving enlightenment, and not only on the use of drugs. To close all avenues because of the dangers involved is like saving "the toenail of society by amputating its foot." In Osmond's words: "We need not put out the visionary's eyes because we do not share his vision. We need not shout down the voice of the mystic because we cannot hear it, or force our rationalizations on him for our own reassurances." [4] Yet this is what has been happening in the past through the various idolatrous worships I have described. Moreover, the present fight against the use of drugs is neither more enlightened nor less foolish than the solution proposed by the fictitious Mmv. To oppose all nontherapeutic use of drugs is to fail to recognize the value and usefulness of drugs as a means of awareness. Furthermore, to oppose such use of drugs without, at the same time, making available to our young other avenues of enlightenment is simply to continue to thwart a natural, legitimate, deep-seated, human urge.

In addressing oneself to the so-called drug problem, one must first get hold of *the whole truth* about drug use, not just the medical and legal aspects of it. One must realize what is obvious to every drug user and student of the religious history of mankind, namely, that the hallucinogenic drug-induced experience *does* have a religious quality. To continue to ignore and deny this is to disseminate ignorance, and drug users know better than to believe such statements. As Geller and Boas write:

Three hundred to six hundred micrograms of LSD take the individual to the profound levels of what has been termed the religious or mystical experience. In this state he may feel "a great love for all things in the cosmos" and a "oneness with God." [5]

When the evidence accumulated through serious research supports the fact that drug users report "a mystical or religious experience, an illumination similar to Zen Satori, and a sense of complete psychological integration," [6] it seems unjustifiable to deny it with the forlorn hope that, by not admitting it, by not recognizing the attractiveness of the drug-induced experience, youngsters will give up the use.

I have heard adults often ask: "What do they want? What kind of awareness are they after? What is there to see that we do not already see?" I think, in answer to this query, that we should humbly realize that many of us have simply lost the ability to appreciate forms of awareness other than those colored green with the dollar sign stamped clearly on them. This is a shortcoming, but to refuse to accept this shortcoming, and to turn viciously against those who are striving to obtain a modicum of awareness of nonordinary reality, is but a form of childish temper tantrum.

More importantly, since drug use, as I have claimed, is primarily symptomatic, we should question ourselves *about the cause itself*. What is it we have been doing to our children when we have denied to them easy access to meaningful experiences? How have we shortchanged them to the extent that drugs are the only means they know for "turning on"? To smother the problem with millions of dollars in research and conferences is not enough. Creating hundreds of committees all over the country to study and report will not get us any farther, as long as we remain concerned only with the symptom. Neither is it enough to continue to print millions of copies of Government reports on the technicalities and dangers of drug use, a practice that simply puffs up the ego of the Idol of Science.

Surely we should help the addict. We should have programs designed to help him rehabilitate himself, and no effort and ingenuity should be spared here. But that is not the whole of the drug problem. Moreover, when the drug problem is viewed in its totality, addiction, terrible though it is, is not the most basic problem. *The fundamental consideration is the denial of an area of human experience.* Any program designed to solve the drug problem must address itself primarily to this area. The programmatic remarks contained in this chapter address themselves almost exclusively to this concern.

To speak first in general terms, it seems to me that one thing we must do is stop denigrating and hindering youth's pursuit of values and larger-than-man concerns. In Roszak's words, "we must insist that a culture which negates or subordinates or degrades visionary experience commits the sin of diminishing our existence." [7] We must stop ridiculing that view of the world and of human beings which is not strictly scientific. We must arrest our blind worship of the Idol of Objectivity, the itch to quantify everything, and, above all, the tendency to redefine things so that they can be quantified. We must stop this reductionism gone berserk.

This is a monumental task. A large part of the machinery of our complex way of living rests on the technology we have developed, and this technology in turn rests on the scientific research and the scientific discoveries we have made and continue to make. Even military superiority depends to a great extent on the military uses to which science can be put. So the questions involved are complex, but they cannot be avoided. At stake is what we want to be. Do we want to be a nation of technocrats, whose attainments are measurable, and measurable in terms of the number of atomic warheads stored in its arsenals, in terms of its automobiles, in terms of its mechanical toys, in terms of its gadgetry—so that, in truth, as Aldous Huxley wrote in fable, our age should be reckoned in terms of "the years of Our Ford"? Or do we want to be a nation recognized primarily for its humanistic achievements? Not that both achievements, the technological and the humanistic, are mutually exclusive and irreconcilable. But because of the way the technical has predominated in our culture to the present day, there has been comparatively little and true humanistic achievement. For what are we respected in the world—for our culture, or for our arms and dollars? Do we wish this to continue, or do we wish it changed? I think the answer to this question is intimately and inextricably connected with the answer one gives to the question of drug use.

To take this one step farther, I would say we must foster and even facilitate a deeper understanding of the reality of human life, a more sincere concern for values, meaning, the religious elements of the Western traditions—in short, the whole realm of the nonrational. Most of the religious experience, whether drug induced or not, occurs at a nonverbal level, and any deliberate overintellectualization would obviously stand in the way of awareness and realization.[8] We must also, in ourselves, understand that he who has opened himself to the dimensions of the nonordinary, and who has allowed himself to be possessed by this stark beauty, will not be likely to place a particularly high value on scientific or technological progress for its own sake.[9]

But besides these tasks which fall to all of us as members of society, there is an institution which bears great responsibility for dealing with this problem at the level of the underlying causes I have identified. This institution is the school—yes, *the public school*. There are two primary roles I see the schools playing in this connection, and they can be classified under the headings of *experience* and of *meaning categories*. I shall explain both in some detail.

1. THE PUBLIC SCHOOL AND THE RELIGIOUS EXPERIENCE

In the first place, in the tenor of all that has been said so far it must be clear that I am considering the religious experience as valuable in itself. In fact, it should be clear that it is precisely the disinterested character of this experience that renders it suspicious to those who cannot conceive of anything that is not useful to something else. It is this disinterested character that makes the experience a threat to a mode of life built so exclusively on profit, on usefulness. So I do consider this experience as having value in itself, for its own sake. I also view it as an experience corresponding to man's instinct for completeness. It should also be made clear that in speaking about the role of the public schools vis-à-vis the religious experience I continue to think it highly proper and expedient to maintain a separation between the two *institutions* of church and state. I am not advocating the obliteration or removal of this distinction.

What I want to propose is that the school become more seriously responsible for the religious quality of experience. Why? Syllogistically, my answer may be stated as follows: One of the primary functions of the school is to facilitate the integration of all the dimensions of experience. But a religious quality (as described in this book) is one of the dimensions of experience. Therefore it is one of the primary functions of the school to facilitate the integration of the religious dimension of experience. This argument must now be explicated.

That one of the primary tasks of the school is to facilitate the integration of experience means that the school is to furnish the child with both tools and opportunities to integrate all the elements and dimensions of his social experience. I do not see how this statement can be open to question. Whatever other tasks we may assign the school, and however we choose to call them, it seems to me undeniable that the schools are primarily designed to engage in an effort to help the young learn to lead a self-satisfying and useful life within society. Such a life is but a complex of experiences encountered at various levels, in varying degrees of intensity, suffused with different qualities. The school helps the child to live his life, as a social being, in a manner that leads to his own self-realization and, at the same time, contributes to the general welfare. Such a school, if it does its job properly, would be, as the saying goes, relevant. Whenever the schools have ceased, in whatever measure and for whatever reason, to help the child achieve this integration, we have had a school system isolated from society's life and interests, turned irrelevant to the social needs of their charges.

Writing in his *The School and Society,* John Dewey maintains that "from the standpoint of the child, the great waste in the school comes from his inability to utilize the experiences he gets outside the school in any complete and free way within the school itself; while, on the other hand, he is unable to apply in daily life what he is learning at school." [10] And again, in still more pertinent terms:

> The child is one, and he must either live as an integral unified being or suffer loss and create friction. To pick up one of the manifold relations which the child bears, and to define the work of the school with relation to that, is like instituting a vast and complicated system of physical exercise which would have for its object simply the development of the lungs and the power of breathing, independent of other organs and functions. The child is an organic whole, intellectually, socially, and morally, as well as physically. The ethical aim which determines the work of the school must accordingly be interpreted in the most comprehensive and organic spirit. We must take the child as a member of society in the broadest sense and demand whatever is necessary to enable the child to recognize all his social relations and to carry them out.[11]

One can hardly find a stronger statement. Yet we have continued to isolate from the school a particular aspect or dimension of the child's social experiences, the religious quality. From the point of view of experience, the religious quality cannot justifiably be excluded from *any* school, public or private. Whenever experience is "interpreted in the most comprehensive and organic spirit," no dimension or quality can be justifiably left out. The principle of separation between church and state is not a sufficient justification for this exclusion, for it concerns the separation of institutions, not the totality of human experience.

When placing the religious quality of experience within the child's social life I do not mean to say that there is a religious dimension to the child's social life just because the child must inevitably meet the religious as he goes with his parents to church or synagogue, or as elements of the various religious traditions meet him through custom and festival. This is, no doubt, part of the child's social experience, and the school must be concerned with it, but it is not the most important consideration. What I have in mind goes somewhat deeper. I mean to say that the adolescent, as he goes through his identity crisis and as he seeks integrating experiences, does not isolate himself from the societal matrix in which his life is lived: as I have noted earlier, the identity crisis *is* social too. The adolescent going through this period of his life does not slough off his crisis as he walks daily through the portals of the school. The dialectics of his life process play themselves continually, no matter where he is. In fact, the schools are an important element in his struggle for identity insofar as in and through them the reigning ideologies are presented to him in all their force and rigidity, and insofar as the rejection, more or less covert, of these ideologies implies also the rejection of the schools. This being the case, the schools can no more ignore the adolescent's need for new horizons and life syntheses than they can ignore him as a human social being.

But it is one thing to say that the elements of the religious experience cannot—or, rather, *should* not—be excluded, and quite another to suggest ways in which such elements can be incorporated into the work of the public school. To this task I now turn.

First of all, there are things that can be done at the level of cognition, but that contribute to the integration of the religious experience into the total social life of the child.

One such thing is the teaching "about" religion, a possibility we all talk about and do nothing about. To be sure, we do not have sufficiently well trained teachers to handle this area of learning, but this is not an insurmountable difficulty. Teaching about religion, about the various religious traditions within Western civilization, is a very necessary thing for the suppression of bias and for the fostering of understanding in our culture and society. This is especially needed today, it seems to me, precisely because through its neglect in the past there is now a woeful ignorance about our Western religious traditions, especially about the more mystical ones.

Besides this, in a negative way, it would be helpful if, for once, we stopped ridiculing the religious traditions in which we live. We are very much aware today of the various psychological influences exerted on children in our schools. We are aware of the deleterious effects that harsh criticisms or lack of appreciation can have on a child's creative endeavors. The same applies to his ability to experience life and the universe religiously. In this respect, one can almost say that more harm is done by the snickering and insensitive teacher than by the openly antagonistic teachers, the self-styled atheists. It would also help if we stopped hindering the expression of the religious sentiment in art, poetry, literature, and in the contemplation of the marvels of nature. We educate by means of the environments that we create, and we teachers are part of these environments. Our actions and reactions—the total interactive process in which we, teachers and pupils, children and adults, are involved—cannot but have either a healthy or a sickening effect on our children. The least we can do in this respect is not be obstructive.

In a more positive sense, however, we can foster in the

child the ability to experience the universe religiously. This we cannot do directly. One cannot teach experience, no matter of what kind. But we can foster the development of the feelings that characterize the religious experience, and we do this in an indirect way by fostering feelings akin to those of a religious experience, such as the feelings of awe, wonder, reverence, vitality. Such are the feelings accompanying imagination, playfulness, sensitivity to and awareness of the world that constantly addresses us in myriad ways,[12] the sense of wonder, hope, humor.[13] If one were to pick a particularly relevant feeling that is akin to the religious feeling, it would be the feeling of wonder, a wonder that originates and sustains the pursuit of understanding, in depth, of events, people, nature, artifacts, ideas, everything. There is, of course, no question of excluding any study of those very things, for study per se is not destructive of wonder. There is no question, either, of introducing a new subject matter into the curriculum. It is primarily a question of communicating and fostering an attitude with regard to everything that is studied or encountered. This is the attitude that persistently seeks ultimate meanings in everything,[14] that continuously displays "an 'infinite care' in the affairs of men" [15]—*care,* the Heideggerian *Sorge* for the "To-Be" of being.[16]

None of these is directly taught. Such attitudes are "caught" when experienced performers display them. We do not teach these attitudes, but children do learn them. In the words of Rudolf Otto:

> There is, of course, no "transmission" of it [the religious sense] in the proper sense of the word; it cannot be "taught," it must be "awakened" from the spirit. And this could not justly be asserted, as it often is, of religion as a whole and in general, for

in religion there *is* very much that *can* be taught—
that is, handed down in concepts and passed on in
school instruction. What is incapable of being so
handed down is this numinous basis and background
to religion, which can only be induced, incited, and
aroused. This is least of all possible by mere verbal
phrase or external symbol; rather we must have recourse to the way all other moods and feelings are
transmitted, to a penetrative imaginative sympathy
with what passes in the other person's mind. More of
the experience lives in reverent attitude and gesture,
in tone and voice and demeanour, expressing its mo-
mentousness.[17]

In brief, if we want our children to stop using drugs, we
must make available to them other means of "turning on."
One way of making sure that the means are available is to
help our children get to know about these means. These
are the means, traditional and otherwise, that have been
present and used within our Western religious traditions.
Teaching "about" religion, therefore, ought to include
teaching about these traditions. Teaching "about" religion,
also, ought to be a very important aspect or part of every
curriculum. Furthermore, one must strive to develop, even
indirectly, the feelings that characterize a religious experience. The fact that these can be "taught" only indirectly
makes it a more difficult, yet none the less essential, task to
perform. In conclusion, one can say that whenever there is
honest and sincere recognition of the value, richness, and
ineffableness of the fullness of experience, the conditions
have been created for the cultivation of the religious attitude. Depth conjures up depth.

2. THE RELIGIOUS AS SOURCE OF
MEANING CATEGORIES

As worthwhile as the religious experience is in itself as a satisfaction of the instinct for completeness, it still has a further role to play that falls squarely within this very function of completion. This is the role of providing a source of meaning categories through which the individual may discover worth where before he saw mere routine and boredom, meaninglessness, chaos, and great irrelevance—or where he simply saw nothing of importance. In describing the way in which a transcendental experience can be a source of meaning categories, Professor Phenix writes as follows:

> The most promising approach to education with religious depth is to combine "secular" and "sacred" materials by using the latter as means of interpreting the ultimate meanings of the former. Traditional religious concepts often provide valuable insights into the fundamental significance of worldly affairs. They have this power because they originally grew out of the need to understand the deeper meanings in certain types of crucial real-life situations, involving such problems as guilt, isolation, hostility, and fear of death, and such affirmative responses as gratitude, love, wonder, and hope. Worldly affairs need the illumination that religious symbols often provide, and traditional religious concepts, in turn, need the secular context in which to exemplify their relevance.[18]

Here, as before, there is no question of eliminating the distinction between the institutions of church and state. Furthermore, there is no question of eliminating the distinction between the sacred and the secular realms, as I have said above, on a *horizontal* level. This distinction is commendable and it has its advantages. But if not at the horizontal level, there is no reason why we should maintain a separation at the *vertical* plane. Such a separation would simply militate against the discovery of meaning in the ordinary experiences of day-to-day living. We should therefore not just allow, but positively encourage, a vertical impregnation of the secular by the sacred, a penetration of the dull veil of the secular by eyes lighted by a new awareness, which can thus perceive unimagined vistas in things that are not on their face holy.[19]

It must be noted that this is a matter not only of conceptual structure but also of feeling based on experience. Millions of words and incantations about the marvels of the atomic age cannot convey what a moment of transcendent lucidity can. And once this has occurred, the experience can bathe life with a new luster, wider horizons can open before our eyes, and we may learn once more to wonder.

3. THE PSYCHEDELIC TEACHER

The key to the suggestions I have been making is, of course, the teacher—not just any teacher, and very probably not the kind of teacher who comes out of our schools of education. The reason such institutions are unequal to the task of turning out the kind of teacher required is simple. Our schools of education are interested only in turning out people who know the subject or subjects they are expected to teach, and all the methodologies necessary for teaching them. While this objective is not per se objectionable, it becomes so when it is the *only* objective in the preparation of teachers. That this is so is obvious to anyone acquainted with the curricula and practices of teacher-preparing institutions. If further confirmation and justification of these statements is needed, I suggest that one read some of the recent critical literature on the schools, especially Silberman's *Crisis in the Classroom*. Moreover, the drug problem itself is proof of the inadequacy of teachers. If teachers were excellent, the drug problem wouldn't be epidemic. In fact, drugs may be needed by many youngsters precisely in order to reverse the deleterious consequences that usually follow the mind-altering experiences to which children are submitted in kindergarten and first grade.[20] The worship of science, neutrality, objectivity, and "facts" demands prodigious tithes. As Michael Murphy writes:

> In America most persons would rather conquer the moon then explore the worlds of subjective experience and personal relationship.
>
> Nowhere is this attitude more obvious than in our educational system. Upon entering school, our children must adapt to the various demands of classroom efficiency. They are taught to behave "normally," to think rationally and objectively, to relate verbally, and to control rather than cultivate their feelings. They may graduate as good citizens, well educated in the cognitive disciplines and well prepared to function as components in society, yet be strikingly unaware of themselves and others.
>
> Such is the price, some say, of our progress. Others, however, are now declaring that the price may not be worth paying. On college campuses throughout America, students are demanding that they be taught not only to think, but also to feel. Many of them are insisting that a basic concern for ultimate values be

added to their curricula and are turning meanwhile to psychedelic drugs.[21]

Some school reform is already taking place, but it may not be enough to stem the tides of indignation at the murderous denial of humanity being perpetrated on our children. I feel reasonably certain that we are now presiding over the demise of the American public school system, and that for some time to come our children will relish the freedom to be children and human that we ourselves did not enjoy. But the withering of the school will not mean the passing away of the teacher. Now, and in the future, the great need is for excellent teachers, psychedelic teachers.

The psychedelic teacher is one who is able to unveil the dimensions of the human soul. He is able to present himself to his students as a human being and to stimulate in them feelings of security and trust, the warmth of friendship and companionship, the solidarity that arises out of a destiny shared. He is a man for whom facts are facts, and for whom what matters is understanding. He knows that he does not know, and he is not afraid or ashamed to say so, yet he lives passionately searching for wisdom and is thus, truly, a philosopher, that is, a friendly wooer of *sophia*. He has understood, not merely conceptually, but in the inner recesses of his being, that wisdom is a communal pursuit. He believes with Plato that only "after much converse about the matter itself and a life lived together, suddenly a light, as it were, is kindled in one soul by a flame that leaps to it from another, and thereafter sustains itself." [22] His artistic sensitivity has been refined so that he can find beauty and aesthetic satisfaction amid the most ordinary experiences of life. He is not jealous of the beauty he discovers, but yearns to enjoy it together with others, mindful of Cicero's comment that beauty is enhanced by sharing.[23] As a true artist, he strives to create beauty together with his students, and he longs for the rare moments when the sublime breaks forth in their midst. He is, finally, enthusiastic, that is, filled with the divine, possessed by the transcendent—he is the "interpreter of the gods," as Plato would say [24]—and he is able to evoke in others intimations of the beyond. Every fact, for him, is a clue, and he is capable of making his pupils "dreamers of what is true." [25]

Such a teacher would of course be more than just knowledgeable in a specialty, or trained in one discipline, or an expert practitioner, though he would undoubtedly be all these and more. He would be educated, in the fullest sense of the term.[26] He would be mentally healthy, balanced, prudent, lest he "succumb to the temptations and threats peculiar to the guiding situation" [27] in which he constantly leads his life. He would be experienced in the dimension of transcendence, and he would have reflected seriously on his experiences so as to be able to guide others and help them cope with the mysteries of the beyond. He would also be able to create a loving environment wherein the pursuit of awareness could be joyfully carried out.

How is the teacher to do all this? What techniques, if any, is he to employ? In the first place, he must be able to create a nice, congenial atmosphere. I have remarked earlier about the importance of the "setting" in the conduct of a drug experience, and on the emphasis given this factor by the religious and monastic traditions in East and West. The same importance must be attributed to the creation of environments wherein both teachers and students may feel at peace with themselves, secure, loved. Masters and Houston are emphatic about the need for such a milieu. They write:

An important function of the guide is to arrange a comfortable, pleasant setting in which the subject's experience will be favorably, and certainly not negatively, influenced by his environment. Such a major role does the physical environment play in determining the course of a subject's experience that it would be difficult to overemphasize the need for this objective climate to be favorable.[28]

Need one insist, in this connection, that the antiseptic schools (or the dilapidated ones) that our children attend are the least likely places for relaxed and meaningful transactions? Whether indoors or outdoors, therefore, the setting must be comfortable, natural, safe, leading to feelings of security, relaxation, harmony, and peace.

Secondly, the teacher must have at his command a variety of meditative, introspective, and questioning techniques to help him guide his pupils in their search for expanded consciousness and transcendental experiences. These techniques, however, cannot be learned in the abstract. Or, perhaps better, they *can* be learned in the abstract, and that is a danger, for when so learned they remain useless and ineffective in the hands of the guide. As I have indicated above, the teacher must guide out of the wealth of his own experience, for which it is needed that he make himself acquainted, conceptually and experientially, with the techniques, ancient as well as modern, that facilitate the flight to the beyond. These techniques include Yoga and Zen as well as Western meditative practices. They also include questioning (or guided meditation) techniques such as those used by Jean Houston in her training of clinical psychologists.[29]

Coupled with the use of techniques—and indeed permeating the entire life of the psychedelic teacher—must go

an effort to focus attention on, or direct it to, unfamiliar
or usually unnoticed aspects or dimensions of "ordinary"
reality.[30] As Wordsworth writes in "The Tables Turned,"

> One impulse from a vernal wood
> May teach you more of man,
> Of moral evil and of good,
> Than all the sages can.

The trouble is that many of us live encased in a conceptual armor whose task is to ward off the fullness of reality.[31] Science presides over the conceptual enclosure beyond which we do not dare venture, within which we have
been captive from childhood, and to which we resolutely
confine our children from their tenderest years, chaining
them "by the leg and also by the neck, so that they cannot
move and can see only what is in front of them, because
the chains will not let them turn their heads." [32] This is the
kingdom of Laputa [33] presided over by the "Whore Reason," wherein we "recognize as reality nothing but the
shadows," [34] for we do not even suspect that what we deem
"our world" is but a small fragment of it. For "thought is
but a part of life and a part cannot grasp the whole. . . .
Thought can grasp the thought of life. Life itself evades its
grasp." [35] The reason, in Bergson's words, is that *the in-
tellect is characterized by a natural inability to comprehend
life.*" [36] Because of this natural inability, in Wordsworth's
words,

> Our meddling intellect
> Misshapes the beauteous forms of things.

The task, then, is to break through the conceptual barriers and misunderstandings about life in which most of our
life has transpired, and to help our children break loose

from the "meaningless illusion" (in Plato's words) that reality is contained by the darkness of a cave.

This task involves the surrender to unaccustomed feelings such as wonder, "the characteristic emotion of the love of wisdom, for such love begins in wonder," [37] and it is continued and perpetuated in it.[38] I say surrender, because I believe a certain amount of passivity is necessary for reality to communicate itself to us. We must be at peace, as it were, and in unhurried leisure, in order to sense the meaning of the rustling of the leaves. If one talks all the time, one cannot hear oneself addressed. Yet as Buber remarks, we are being addressed all the time by events, by people, by things. The question is to hear, to be attentive. I think de Madariaga expresses this well when he writes:

> While I believe less and less that we can grasp "nature," I believe more and more that, at least at fleeting moments, we may feel, experience, taste it. This privilege goes by the name of grace. It may come to the saint or to the artist. It may come to any human being who lives a moment of sanctity or of inspiration. These moments are rare, intimate, profound, and apt to be protected by a mist of shyness. The favored one is not likely to speak about them. They may be more frequent than meets the eye or the ear.
>
> Were I therefore asked whether the philosopher or the scientist on the one hand or the saint or the poet on the other can get closer to the Mystery, I should not hesitate, for the philosopher and the scientist endeavor to penetrate the Mystery, while the saint and the poet let themselves be penetrated by it. . . .
>
> This is another lesson learned in life: Thou must know how to remain passive before the world. Let the soul hollow itself in the shape of a riverbed for

life to flow undisturbed by the untutored movements
of the self, and the vital flow will vivify the riverbed
and make it feel and taste that which is.[39]

The surrender to the expansive consciousness of life
must not be thought, on the other hand, to constitute a
threat to scientific, philosophical, or technological development. This would be a terrible misunderstanding. The task
is not *only* to feel, or *only* to understand, but to understand
feelingly. This is, I think, what Buber has in mind in his
example of the tree. In considering a tree, one can dwell on
its aesthetic impact, the colors, the background, the movement; one can also appreciate it as a marvelous example of
organic interaction with the environment; one can study it
botanically, classify it, name it; one can even compress it
into number, as an expression of fundamental laws of energy and growth. But, Buber adds,

> It can . . . also come about, if I have both will and
> grace, that in considering the tree I become bound
> up in relation to it. The tree is no longer *It*. I have
> been seized by the power of exclusiveness.
>
> To effect this it is not necessary for me to give up
> any of the ways in which I consider the tree. There
> is nothing from which I would have to turn my eyes
> away in order to see, and no knowledge that I would
> have to forget. Rather is everything, picture and
> movement, species and type, law and number, in-
> divisibly united in this event.[40]

The same truly holistic experience is encountered in
Teilhard de Chardin's narrative about his visit to the University of California's cyclotrons. There, as he saw world
processes mirrored or reproduced in the cyclotrons, an experience which, as he says, might have made his head reel,
all that he felt, on the contrary, "was . . . peace and joy,

a *fundamental* peace and joy." [41] I think this is also the way in which one must think of Kepler, studying the movements of the planets and seeing them as

> nothing except a certain everlasting polyphony (intelligible, not audible) with dissonant tunings, like certain syncopations or cadences (wherewith men imitate these natural dissonances), which tends towards fixed and prescribed clauses—the single clauses having six terms (like voices)—and which marks out and distinguishes the immensity of time with those notes. Hence it is no longer a surprise that man, the ape of his Creator, should finally have discovered the art of singing polyphonically, which was unknown to the ancients, namely, in order that he might play the everlastingness of all created time in some short part of an hour by means of an artistic concord of many voices and that he might to some extent taste the satisfaction of God the Workman with His own works, in that very sweet sense of delight elicited from this music which imitates God.[42]

This is *care* for reality, the finding of infinite depths of meaning in everything. This is what the psychedelic teacher must help his pupils achieve. The warmth of his enthusiasm, of his "divine possession," must kindle in them the desire to see, to turn themselves around, to "convert" themselves and slowly grow accustomed to the new dimensions of reality. This is, indeed, an art.[43]

Yet, in the exercise of this art there must be no compulsion. One must present oneself as a guide because one has been over the terrain before, and one knows of its perils and rewards. It is thus that Vergil gave himself to Dante as a guide. One must present oneself as a master because one has mastered certain techniques that now form part of one's life, which is therefore a model worth imitating. One must present oneself as a teacher because one has acquired certain knowledges that may be worth communicating to others. Yet one must only present oneself, without any gesture of interference, for it is up to the student to accept or reject, to change, to reinterpret, to reject today and accept tomorrow. The vision that quickens the teacher and integrates his own life will flow out of him as long as he is sincere, and it will have the power of integrating the pupil's life only if it is not imposed, if it is acceptable in freedom.[44]

This is the ideal of the psychedelic teacher. But how does one practice this ideal? Supposing one *is* becoming such a person, how does one practice all this in the midst of one's teaching of literature, geography, math? Basically, by using each of the disciplines as so many elements to be integrated, as pieces of a puzzle, as so many clues to further syntheses, as materials to be "informed" with coherence.

The model here is derived from Michael Polanyi's *The Tacit Dimension*. For Polanyi, reality is ontologically composed of that which immediately appears plus that to which it points. He defines reality as "something that attracts our attention by clues which harass and beguile our minds into getting ever closer to it." [45] At a phenomenological level, this entails the apprehension of the clues as functional, that is, as entities whose function is to point to the realities that lie beyond, to realities that are present but hidden. Polanyi calls the clues *proximal* and the hidden meanings *distal*.

One implication of this model is, of course, that no picture of reality is ever complete if it concerns itself solely with the immediately visible, the proximal. The rampant scientific positivism of our day, as I have been maintaining, is but a caricature of reality.[46] The point, then, is to use school learnings as functional, as proximal symbols and clues of a reality that, though distal, is required in order to give them fullness of meaning and ontic completion. The scientific disciplines in this way lose their finality and exclusiveness, and teaching puts on the interpretive character it has lacked for so long. "Don't look at me," says the psychedelic teacher; "look where I am looking by means of these disciplines."

It must be noted that nothing in this model suggests that the disciplines ought not to be studied thoroughly, in themselves. On the contrary, the model requires that they be studied in depth, for only out of these depths can their full symbolic nature be discerned. What Phenix writes about the knowledge of God is equally applicable in this case. Only by a deep understanding of nature, events, people, artifacts, and ideas does one eventually begin to fathom the immense possibilities of the distal, the transcendent.[47]

The model, however, does suggest that the study of the proximal is not terminal. The aim, the goal, is to use the proximal *functionally,* to enjoy the coherences to which it points and within which alone it can be fully comprehended. It is at this point that the proximal becomes *tacit* and yields itself functionally to the fascinations of the transcendent. What we require is the "enthusiasm and pedagogical mysticism" [48] of the psychedelic teacher.

Perhaps an example or two will make this process clear. Think of the accomplished pianist who decides to learn a Beethoven sonata he has never played before. In front of his eyes, on the piano stand, is the music, all the notes and dynamic markings, instructions, perhaps even fingering suggestions. The tedious task of learning begins, the process of routinizing, habituating the fingers to the intricate patterns of *this* particular sonata. This is the stage in which concern with the proximal in itself is paramount. This stage cannot be dispensed with, as any good pianist knows. But obviously the pianist's objective is to play the music, to re-create an aesthetic experience in himself and in his audience. As the fingering and the techniques of expression become habit, the pianist's concern shifts away from it to the musical interpretation, the musical presentation. He no longer focuses his attention on his hands, on the fingering, but on the music as a whole. The dimension of the proximal, in fact, has become tacit, for the sake of the attention demanded by the distal.

In the same way, when we acquire a second language as adults, we learn to attend to meaning only after we have habituated ourselves to the peculiar sounds of letters and words in the new language.

One must note here that in many instances we are first reached by the distal without any explicit reliance on the proximal. Thus we appreciate the beauty of a poem even before we have studied its structure, and the impact of a powerful musical performance imposes itself on us often before we have had a chance to study or analyze it. Thus, in the first set of examples, there is a movement from the proximal to the distal; in the second set, the problem is to retain or regain the distal after one undertakes an analysis of its proximal components.

Such, then, are the tasks and methods of the psychedelic teacher. He, more than any*thing* else, is needed by the drug-using generation. The question remains whether such men and women can be found in sufficient numbers. Perhaps more pointedly, the question is whether or not they could function proximally, leading youth to distal and ultimate meanings, within the misanthropic system of school-

EPILOGUE

I would like to conclude this book by restating briefly what I have tried to say—and what I have not said. In the first place, I am not advocating a revivalist LSD religious movement of the kind proposed by Dr. Leary and some of his friends and followers, though I must say that such a movement is quite properly within the traditional lines of religions the world over. I am not claiming, either, that every heroin addict is on his way to sanctity. Neither am I advocating an indiscriminate use of drugs. On the other hand, I cannot agree with Roszak when he states that "there is nothing whatever in common between a man of Huxley's experience and intellectual discipline sampling mescaline, and a fifteen-year-old tripper whiffing airplane glue until his brain turns to oatmeal." [1] Without denying the difference, obvious to everyone, and without denying the importance of the difference, I must point out that basically Huxley and the tripper do have a lot in common, one of the most important common traits being the quest for an all-encompassing experience. This commonality is equally of great importance, and is at the root of the arguments presented here.

It is precisely the quest for a transcendental experience and awareness that I have tried to uncover by calling drug use symptomatic. I have, moreover, maintained that this quest is natural in man, an instinct that seeks completion in the religious experience and the religious feeling. Furthermore, I have maintained that the exaggerated overintellectualization of our technocratic society and way of life has thwarted this instinct for too long, and that our youth, faced as they are with momentous questions never before fathomed by man, are having recourse to just any kind of means in order to break through the barriers we have erected for them. Finally, I have claimed that our youth's deprivation can be corrected, and that the schools, the public schools of this country, do have an important role to play in this reconstruction of the wholeness of human experience.

In the light of what has been said so far, I invite you to read the following newsclip by Edward B. Fiske, which appeared in *The New York Times,* Sunday, May 10, 1970, p. 58. The headline reads, "SURFING HAS BECOME FOR SOME A WAY TO RELIGIOUS EXPERIENCE."

> Michael Hynson, his short, lean figure clad in a black rubber wet suit, sat cross-legged in the sand in the Yoga stance and looked intently out into the Pacific. He meditated quietly for several minutes, then took his surfboard in hand and strove out into the waves.
>
> At 27 years of age, Mr. Hynson is one of the top

surfers in the world. He is also one of a growing number of surfing enthusiasts who in the last few years have begun to talk and write about it not only as a sport but also as a religious discipline.

"Surfing is a spiritual experience," he said. "When you become united with a wave, you lose your identity on one level and make contact with it again on a higher plane."

From Long Island Sound to Hawaii, surfers are turning to what has become known as "soul surfing." Many follow rigorous diets of natural foods as a means of purifying themselves. They meditate regularly, especially before surfing, and see the sea as a way of turning on without drugs.

ALLEGORY OF LIFE

"The younger kids especially see surfing as a way of getting to the roots of their being," said John Severson, editor of *Surfer Magazine*. "They think of the waves as an allegory of life and creation. They feel that when you are in the center of a wave it's like being in the center of the world."

Others, however, while acknowledging the importance of the trend, deplore it as destructive and say it is giving surfing a bad name.

"It's a good clean sport and that's all," said Donald Hansen, the 33-year-old founder and head of Hansen Surfboards, one of the major manufacturers of surfing equipment. "It's not a religion or a way of life. Parents are skeptical about their kids getting into it when they hear about the religious thing."

From ancient times, of course, the sea has been a symbol of life, creation, and other fundamental religious ideas. In Hindu and Buddhist thought, for instance, the wave is a symbol of the individual who rises to life and then disappears back into the universal oneness of reality.

In this country surfing developed as a sport in the early twentieth century and blossomed into a multi-million dollar business after World War II. According to Mr. Severson, the religious dimensions became widely recognized only recently.

One apparent reason for this development is the rising interest in this country, especially among youths, in new religious forms, among them astrology and other forms of the occult.

Yoga, which combines physical conditioning with mental and spiritual discipline, is popular among many surfers, including numerous top international competitors. In virtually all instances, surfers articulate the religious dimensions of their activity in terms of Eastern rather than Western religion and have abandoned any ties with traditional Western religious institutions.

Mr. Severson also believes that the drug scene has been an important spur. "Drugs opened people up to a lot of new possibilities and eliminated a lot of hangups," he stated. "Kids became more tolerant of people thinking for themselves and getting into new and different things."

Mr. Hynson said that his own experience followed this pattern. "I used to be into LSD—not as an escape but as a sacrament, a total sacrament," he said. "Now I've moved on and find that in surfing I still get high and locked into the rhythm of the self. It turns you on to God."

All surfers interviewed agreed that the peak religious experience comes when the individual finds himself at the physical center of the wave—a point they describe as "in the tube" or "in the pocket."

Michael Doyle, 29, who has twice been ranked as the world's leading surfer by *Surfer Magazine,* for instance, reported, "At that point you're aware of a lot more energy. You spin out. You're only there for a few seconds, but you can be high for days."

Mr. Hynson described it as an "energy exchange." "You're there anticipating in the right spot, and then it takes you," he said. "Sometimes I feel like I'm just a vehicle for something. You feel like you're in total harmony with the divine at every level."

Mr. Hansen complained that those who get heavily into the religious dimension of surfing tend to lose their aggressiveness and drop out of organized competition, thus damaging surfing as an industry. "They seem to think they can forget about the commercial side," he said. "Some of us who have developed the sport into what it is now may find ourselves out of business."

Two ideologies have persistently appeared in the preceding pages, and they are very much the subject of discussion in books and articles today. One is the ideology of humanism, deep concern, of search for values, of a quest for religious experiences. The other is the overrationalistic ideology, the concern for the technological at all costs. This latter is represented by the military, business, and industrial concerns of the nation, the former is today almost exclusively the concern of our youth.

In the newspaper article reproduced above, the religious and the business orientations are clearly discernible. The clash depicted in the views of the young surfers and Mr. Hansen is a clear example of the clash we are experiencing in society today, though society faces the clash on many different fronts. The Mr. Hansen referred to is typical of the emphases that predominate in our culture. "The commercial side" is his concern, his only concern, really. He would not hesitate to proscribe completely the "religious dimension of surfing," since it hurts his business, and business, for him—and for so many of us—is the only important consideration.

One would like to ask Mr. Hansen what would happen to the young surfers if they could no longer get high by surfing. If this means were no longer available to them, they might, perhaps, fall back on LSD, or mescaline, or marijuana. But this, of course, is not Mr. Hansen's problem! Neither has it been the business of millions of people who have been deaf to the concern for values and meaningful experiences in their children as these grew up. The danger is that too many still continue to think in the same way.

If you agree with the arguments I have presented here, I have one word for you: exert yourself to create the kind of environment where our young will be able to satisfy their eager quest for transcendental experiences. When such a situation is achieved, the use of drugs as the predominant means for enlightenment will cease.

If, however, you do not agree, let me simply remind you of the evil consequences of misplaced care. A man may die of a ruptured appendix if all you do when he complains of a pain in his side is give him a shot of morphine. Also, it seems unnecessary to maim a man by amputating his foot in order to save his toenail. This is the lesson of the fable of Zzyr. At any rate, such misplaced care was not Zzyr's own idea. It was suggested by Mmv. And Mmv was a fool.

APPENDIXES

APPENDIX I

A Classification of Psychotropic Drugs

The following classification is summarized from *Psychoactive Drugs,* by David E. Smith, Joel Fort, and Delores L. Craton, in *Drug Abuse Papers 1969,* ed. by David E. Smith (2d ed.; Berkeley: Continuing Education in Criminology, University Extension, University of California, 1969).

I. SEDATIVE—HYPNOTICS
   A. Alcohol (in all its forms)
   B. Barbiturates and barbiturate-like drugs (Amytal, Sombucaps, Nembutal, Tuinal, Seconal, phenobarbital, Doriden, etc.)
   C. Tranquilizers (Thorazine, Stelazine, etc.)
   D. *Cannabis sativa* (hashish, marijuana, etc.)

II. NARCOTICS
    A. Opiates (opium, heroin)
    B. Analgesics (morphine, codeine, Demerol, Dolo-
       phine, etc.)
    C. Proprietary preparations (various cough syrups)

III. CENTRAL NERVOUS SYSTEM STIMULANTS
    A. Nicotine (tobacco, in all its forms)
    B. Caffeine (coffee, tea, cola, "No-Doz," etc.)
    C. Cocaine
    D. Amphetamines (Benzedrine, Dexedrine, Dexamyl,
       Biphetamine, Methedrine, Preludin, etc.)
    E. Antidepressants (Ritalin, Flavil, Paranate)

IV. PSYCHEDELICS
    LSD, psilocybin, DMT, STP, mescaline (peyote), PCP
    (Sernyl), morning glory seeds, baby wood rose seeds

APPENDIX II

Distinctions Between Descriptions of Drug-induced and Spontaneous Experiences

Using the very same six passages reproduced in Chapter 2, I asked some of my students, graduate and undergraduate, to answer the following questions by checking as many items as applicable:

I. Which of the preceding narratives describe experiences that are

1. Drug-induced   1___ 2___ 3___ 4___ 5___ 6___
2. Spontaneous   1___ 2___ 3___ 4___ 5___ 6___

II. On what grounds did you differentiate between the drug-induced and the spontaneous experiences?

1. Had known some of the passages _____
2. Followed a hunch, a guess _____

3. No grounds whatsoever _____
4. On the following grounds (specify) _____

The results are given in Table I:

TABLE I

(N = 97)

I.	No.	DRUG-INDUCED	SPONTANEOUS	TOTAL ANSWERS
	1	39%	61%	88
	2	53%	47%	91
	3	14%	86%	87
	4	46%	54%	89
	5	73%	27%	88
	6	46%	54%	88

Total 531

II.   TOTAL ANSWERS

1. Had known passages	6	6%
2. Guessed	53 ⎫	69%
3. No grounds	14 ⎭	
4. Had grounds	18	19%
5. "Impossible to tell"	4 ⎫	
6. "Cannot tell without knowing person"	2 ⎭	6%

N = 97

The following are reasons mentioned by those who said they had discriminated because they had grounds for doing so. The list included also comments from others who said they had guessed:

prior drug experience	4
vocabulary and style	6
coherence of thought	3
depth of feelings	3
imagery	4
otherworldliness	2
	Total = 22

The only significant point is that 73 percent did consider No. 5 to be drug induced (which, in fact, it was), and that 86 percent thought No. 3 was spontaneous (which, in fact, it was). To find an explanation for this positive identification, a breakdown of the 22 answers that listed comments was made. Of these, 73 percent noted No. 5 as drug induced, and 91 percent noted No. 3 as spontaneous. Also 64 percent classified *both* No. 3 and No. 5 correctly.

Given the reasons presented in the 22 answers cited above, it is easy to see why No. 3 was identified as being spontaneous. It is the only one that is sober, devoid of striking imagery. The reverse is true of No. 5. However, the qualities that served here as criteria do not form part of any of the standards enumerated by serious students of mysticism. The only reasonable conclusion seems to be that different criteria would lead to different conclusions. One must not insist that the experiences, as narrated, are simply indistinguishable. They *are* distinguishable, but only through reference to a specific set of criteria.

NOTES

NOTES

INTRODUCTION

1. Allen Geller and Maxwell Boas, *The Drug Beat* (Cowles Book Company, Inc., 1969).

2. Peter Marin and Allan Y. Cohen, *Understanding Drug Use: An Adult's Guide to Drugs and the Young* (Harper & Row, Publishers, Inc., 1971).

3. Theodore X. Barber, *LSD, Marijuana, Yoga, and Hypnosis* (Aldine Publishing Company, 1970).

4. Abram Hoffer and Humphrey Osmond, *The Hallucinogens* (Academic Press, Inc., 1967).

5. Heinrich Klüver, *Mescal and Mechanisms of Hallucinations* (The University of Chicago Press, 1966).

6. David E. Smith (ed.), *Drug Abuse Papers 1969* (2d ed.; Berkeley: Continuing Education in Criminology, University Extension, University of California, 1969).

7. D. E. Smith, *op. cit.,* "Introduction."

8. Hoffer and Osmond, *op. cit.,* p. v.

9. *Ibid.,* pp. 132–133.

CHAPTER 1. THE DRUG PHENOMENON AS SYMPTOM

1. Walter N. Pahnke and William A. Richards, "Implications of LSD and Experimental Mysticism," *Journal of Religion and Health,* Vol. V (1966), p. 176. The full account of Pahnke's fascinating research is contained in his Ph.D. dissertation, "Drugs and Mysticism," Harvard University, 1963.

2. Jean Houston, "Psycho-Chemistry and the Religious Consciousness," *International Philosophical Quarterly,* Vol. V (Spring, 1965), pp. 411–412. The last words correspond almost exactly to the way in which Suzuki describes existential intuition, which, he says, "is different from sense-intuition or from intellectual intuition, both of which are still on the objective plane of thinking and therefore require something standing before the subject. But in the case of what I call existential intuition there is no object, no subject, in the relativistic sense of the terms; there is only an absolute 'is-ness' or rather 'is' which cannot be defined as this or that. It is something which is not a something in which existential intuition takes place. When it sees itself as reflected in itself, there is an intuition." (Daisetz T. Suzuki, *The Essentials of Zen Buddhism;* London: Rider & Co., 1962, p. 45.) As Suzuki explains later (pp. 153 ff.), this existential intuition marks the turning point of total conversion which is *satori.*

3. Jack Kytle, "Better Living Through Chemistry?" *Outside the Net,* No. 1 (Winter, 1970), pp. 12–13.

4. *The President's Advisory Commission on Narcotic and Drug Abuse—Final Report,* Nov. 1963, p. 17.

5. Quoted in *Time,* Feb. 15, 1971, p. 46.

6. Thomas M. Cosgriff, "The Problem of Drug Abuse," *Notre Dame Journal of Education*, Vol. I, No. 4 (Winter, 1971), p. 299.

7. See Paul Ducasse, *A Philosophical Scrutiny of Religion* (The Ronald Press Company, 1953), p. 315.

8. William Braden, *The Private Sea: LSD and the Search for God* (Quadrangle Books, Inc., 1967), p. 20.

9. Cf. Thomas F. O'Dea, *The Sociology of Religion* (Prentice-Hall, Inc., 1966), p. 15.

10. Thomas M. Cosgriff, *loc. cit.*, p. 297.

11. Theodore Roszak, *The Making of a Counter Culture* (Doubleday & Company, Inc., 1969), p. 156.

12. Walter T. Stace, *Mysticism and Philosophy* (J. B. Lippincott Company, 1960), p. 75.

13. Timothy F. Leary and Walter H. Clark, "Religious Implications of Consciousness Expanding Drugs," *Religious Education*, Vol. LVIII, No. 2 (May, 1963), p. 253.

14. Roszak, *op. cit.*, p. 158.

15. Albert Camus, *The Myth of Sisyphus* (Vintage Books, Inc., 1955), p. 41.

16. William James, *The Varieties of Religious Experience* (The New American Library, Inc., Mentor Books, 1958), pp. 297–298. Cf. also Henri Bergson, *The Two Sources of Morality and Religion* (Doubleday & Company, Inc., Anchor Books, 1935), pp. 218 ff. Huston Smith, in "Do Drugs Have Religious Import?" *Journal of Philosophy*, Vol. LXI, No. 18 (1964), pp. 519–520, remarks that "even the Bible notes that chemically induced psychic states bear *some* resemblance to religious ones. Peter had to appeal to a circumstantial criterion—the early hour of the day—to defend those who were caught up in the Pentecostal experience against the charge that they were drunk: 'These men are not drunk, as you suppose, since it is only the third hour of the day' (Acts 2:15); and Paul initiates the comparison when he admonishes the Ephesians not to 'get drunk with wine . . . but to be

filled with the Spirit' (Eph. 5:18)."

17. Alan Watts, *The Book. On the Taboo Against Knowing Who You Are* (Collier Books, 1966), p. 9.

18. G. Stephens Spinks, *Psychology and Religion* (Beacon Press, Inc., 1963), pp. 90 ff.

19. Cf. Pahnke and Richards, *loc cit.,* p. 197.

20. Vernon J. Bourke, *Aquinas' Search for Wisdom* (Bruce Publishing Company, 1965), pp. 192–193.

21. Plato, *Epistle* VII. 341c–d (J. Harward tr.).

22. Examples of this abound. A striking sampling may be found in Roszak, *op. cit.,* pp. 275–289.

23. Cf. Robert Michaelsen, "The Public Schools and 'America's Two Religions,'" *Journal of Church and State,* Vol. VIII (Autumn, 1966), pp. 380–400.

24. Hoffer and Osmond, *op. cit.,* p. 134.

25. Geller and Boas, *op. cit.,* p. x.

26. Pahnke and Richards, *loc. cit.,* pp. 183, 186.

27. Spinks, *op. cit.,* p. 115.

28. This point is well stated by Malcolm R. Wescott, *Toward a Contemporary Psychology of Intuition* (Holt, Rinehart and Winston, Inc., 1968), p. 182: "Exploration of the psychedelic experience itself, in an effort to describe, classify, or explain in the ordinary terms of logic and science, appears to be quite irrelevant. . . . This is not simply an argument that science is unequal to the task; it is an argument that science is not relevant to the task. When we measure painting by the square yard, sculpture by the pound, music by the average frequency per measure—all of which science can do with great precision—we are making statements with firm empirical referents, with clear communication, and with repeatability; when we make measurements of preference for certain acts or measure autonomic arousal contingent upon certain sensory events, or of verbal reports of altered experience, we are also speaking of events with firm empirical referents, though our precision and stability may be somewhat lower.

However, when we speak of the experience of art, the experience of music, or the experience of literature, the measurements we have made above are quite beside the point. Science, as an enterprise, is conducted within a logical system which relies on communicable and shared knowledge of repeatable events. The events which concern us here, whatever they are called, are individual, unique, incommunicable, and are not within the pale of such a system. The 'truth' about psychedelic experience is a long way off, just as the 'truth' about reality is a long way off."

CHAPTER 2. DRUGS AND ULTIMATE CONCERNS

1. Charles A. Reich, *The Greening of America* (Random House, Inc., 1970), p. 168.

2. Stace, *op. cit.*, pp. 29–30.

3. The point here is *not* that the drug-induced experiences cannot be distinguished from spontaneous ones, but that the drug-induced ones would meet any reliable set of criteria devised for separating genuine from pseudomystical experiences. In fact, I have found that it *is* possible to separate the drug-induced experiences from spontaneous ones when the criteria are not specifically formulated. For details, see Appendix II.

4. Christopher Isherwood (ed.), *Bhagavad-Gita* (The New American Library, Inc., Mentor Books, 1944), pp. 91–92.

5. Aldous Huxley, *The Doors of Perception* (London: Chatto & Windus, Ltd., 1954), pp. 12–13.

6. Cf. Joseph F. Conwell, S.J., *Contemplation in Action* (Gonzaga University Press, 1957), p. 29.

7. Pierre Teilhard de Chardin, *Hymn of the Universe* (Harper & Row, Publishers, Inc., 1965), pp. 42–46. The selection reproduced here is taken from my own translation of

the passage as it appeared in *Orientierung,* Vol. XXV (1961), p. 190.

8. James, *The Varieties of Religious Experience,* p. 301, n. 10.

9. Cf. Anne Freemantle, *The Protestant Mystics* (London: George Weidenfeld & Nicolson, Ltd., 1964), pp. 361–362.

10. Rudolf Otto, *The Idea of the Holy* (Galaxy Books, 1958), pp. 8–11.

11. Spinks, *op. cit.,* p. 49.

12. Otto, *op. cit.,* p. 31.

13. *Ibid.,* p. 37.

14. James, *The Varieties of Religious Experience,* p. 383.

15. *Ibid.*

16. Stace, *op. cit.,* pp. 79, 110–111, 131–133.

17. Spinks, *op. cit.,* pp. 161 ff.

18. James, *The Varieties of Religious Experience,* pp. 292–294.

19. Joachim Wach, *Types of Religious Experience, Christian and Non-Christian* (The University of Chicago Press, 1951), pp. 32–33.

20. Pahnke and Richards, *loc. cit.,* pp. 176–183.

21. Smith, *loc. cit.,* p. 526, writes: "Emotionally the drug experience can be like having forty-foot waves crash over you for several hours while you cling desperately to a life-raft which may be swept from under you at any minute. It seems quite possible that such an ordeal, like any experience of a close call, could awaken rather fundamental sentiments respecting life and death and destiny and trigger the 'no atheists in foxholes' effect. Similarly, as the subject emerges from the trauma and realizes that he is not going to be insane as he feared, there may come over him an intensified appreciation like that frequently reported by patients recovering from critical illness."

22. Dom Cuthbert Butler, *Western Mysticism* (2d ed.;

Harper Torchbooks, 1966), p. 240.

23. *Ibid.*, p. 240.

24. Hoffer and Osmond, *op. cit.*, p. 133. See also Pahnke and Richards, *loc. cit.*, pp. 194 ff.

25. Spinks, *op. cit.*, pp. 171–172; Butler, *op. cit.*, pp. 237–238. Speaking about fastings, flagellations, and sensory deprivation, Jean Houston, *loc. cit.*, p. 397, notes that "recent physiological investigation of these practices in a laboratory setting tends to confirm the notion that askesis-provoked alterations in body chemistry and body rhythm are in no small way responsible for the dramatic change in consciousness attendant upon these practices. The askesis of fasting, for example, makes for vitamin and sugar deficiencies which act to lower the efficiency of the cerebral reducing valve. The practice of flagellation will tend to release quantities of histamine, adrenalin, and the toxic decomposition products of protein—all of which will work to induce shock and hallucination."

26. H. Smith, *loc. cit.*, p. 518.

27. Leary and Clark, *loc. cit.*, p. 255. The same can be said about "bad trips." Hoffer and Osmond state (*op. cit.*, p. 98) that "the most remarkable fact about LSD complications is their rarity. They have occurred among the emotionally labile, hysterical, and paranoid subjects," that is, individuals constitutionally predisposed to such imbalances. And even in these instances, most of which are nonclinical, the complications were possibly due not to LSD per se but to still unidentified ergot compounds present in black-market LSD.

28. Butler, *op. cit.*, pp. 227–228.

29. Spinks, *op. cit.*, p. 154.

30. Hoffer and Osmond, *op. cit.*, pp. 104–110, 482.

31. Leary and Clark, *loc. cit.*, p. 252. See also Geller and Boas, *op. cit.*, p. 189.

32. Smith, *loc. cit.*, p. 520.

33. Sidney M. Jourard, "Psychedelic Drugs and the Young: A Social-Phenomenological View," *Notre Dame Journal of Education*, Vol. I, No. 4 (Winter, 1971), p. 312.

34. Leary and Clark, *loc. cit.*, p. 255.

35. Geller and Boas, *op. cit.*, p. 190.

36. Carlos Castaneda, *The Teachings of Don Juán: A Yaqui Way of Knowledge* (Ballantine Books, 1968).

37. Roszak, *op. cit.*, p. 257. See also Alan Watts, *The Joyous Cosmology* (Vintage Books, Inc., 1962), pp. 12–13; Huxley, *op. cit.*, p. 58.

38. See Geller and Boas, *op. cit.*, p. 187. Also Martin Buber, *Between Man and Man* (The Macmillan Company, 1965), pp. 10–13; Eric Berne, *Games People Play* (Grove Press, Inc., 1964), pp. 178 ff.

39. Roszak, *op. cit.*, p. 223.

40. William James, "The Sentiment of Rationality," in Alburey Castell (ed.), *William James, Essays in Pragmatism*, (Hafner Pub. Co., Inc., 1948), p. 7.

41. Walter Houston Clark, *Chemical Ecstasy: Psychedelic Drugs and Religion* (Sheed & Ward, Inc., 1969), p. 78. H. Smith, *loc. cit.*, pp. 529–530, writes: "The conclusion to which evidence currently points would seem to be that chemicals *can* aid the religious life, but only where set within a context of faith (meaning by this the conviction that what they disclose is true) and discipline (meaning diligent exercise of the will in an attempt to work out the implications of the disclosures for the living of life in the everyday life in the everyday, commonsense world)."

42. Butler, *op. cit.*, p. 146.

43. Other confirmations abound. For an insightful analysis of the relevance of character changes induced by the use of LSD, see " 'Speed Freaks' vs. 'Acid Heads,' " in D. E. Smith (ed.), *op. cit.*

44. James, *The Varieties of Religious Experience,* p. 389. See also Butler, *op. cit.*, pp. 146 ff.; John Dewey, *A Common Faith* (Yale University Press, 1968), p. 171.

45. James, *The Varieties of Religious Experience,* pp. 33–34; Clark, *op. cit.,* p. 84.

46. Aldous Huxley, "Readings in Mysticism," in Christopher Isherwood (ed.), *Vedanta* (London: George Allen & Unwin, Ltd., 1948), pp. 376–377. See also Spinks, *op. cit.,* pp. 172–173.

47. James, *The Varieties of Religious Experience,* p. 191.

48. Jourard, *loc. cit.,* p. 316. Cf. also H. Smith, *loc. cit.,* p. 529.

49. Plato, *Republic* vii. 515.

50. Plato, *Republic* vii. 519.

51. Augustine, *De Civ. Dei* xix. 19.

52. Suzuki, *op. cit.,* pp. 252 ff.

53. Spinks, *op. cit.,* pp. 152–153.

54. By this I do not mean to say that there is just one, and only one, religious instinct. Indeed, it may well be that it is a very complex one. See Gordon W. Allport, *The Individual and His Religion* (The Macmillan Company, 1960), pp. 7 ff. The important point is that there is an instinctual propensity, single- or many-faceted, that impels man to seek completeness.

55. Cf. José M. R. Delgado, *Emotions* (Wm. C. Brown Company, 1966), p. 16.

56. Erich Fromm, *Psychoanalysis and Religion* (Yale University Press, 1967), p. 26. See also Spinks, *op. cit.,* pp. 48 ff.

57. Erich Fromm, *Man for Himself* (Fawcett World Library, 1967), p. 55.

58. Camus, *The Myth of Sisyphus,* p. 13.

59. To be sure, many think they have found psychological substitutes in science or other secular experiences. I doubt that any fully secularized society can exist. The problem entails, simply, the difference between the Holy and those things to which men relate as if they were holy. If by theism one means belief in a transcendent reality, then, obviously, denial of transcendence would make the one who denies it *ipso facto* an atheist. In this sense there obviously are atheists. But if by theism is meant a belief in some absolute that transcends in-

dividual human experience, then I do not believe there can be atheists. In this sense the atheist is simply the one who makes his own gods, the idolater. See H. Paissac, O.P., "Athéisme chez les chrétiens," *Vie Spirituelle, Supplement,* I (1947), pp. 5–28.

Talking about his own experience, Ignace Lepp writes: "With me communism played a role that, psychologically speaking, was not unlike the role religion plays in the lives of believers. . . . My firm conviction, a conviction that I felt no need to express in words, was that life in this world constitued a self-sufficient totality that needed no finality nor justification outside or above the terrestrial. But the reality which I designated by the word 'world' took on so broad and complex a meaning that it almost matched in intensity the Christian's hope in eternal life. . . . Almost all Communists grow angry when they are told that their communism serves them as a religion. This is because the word 'religion' connotes something theological, a totality of beliefs that are not 'scientifically' justified. Nevertheless, it is a psychological fact that the militant and sincere Communist conducts himself exactly like a religious believer. . . . For me and for many of my comrades, communism denoted something almost mystical, although we all would have protested against such a designation, so pejorative a sense did the word have in our circles. . . . Existentially, the subjective transcendence communism provided for me performed exactly the same psychological function as divine transcendence." (Ignace Lepp, *Atheism in Our Time,* pp. 26, 27, 29, 30; The Macmillan Company, 1964.)

60. Spinks, *op. cit.,* pp. 49–50.

61. Erik H. Erikson, *Childhood and Society* (2d ed.; W. W. Norton & Company, Inc., 1963), p. 261.

62. Erik H. Erikson, *Young Man Luther* (W. W. Norton & Company, Inc., 1958), p. 14.

63. Erik H. Erikson, *Identity, Youth and Crisis* (W. W. Norton & Company, Inc., 1968), p. 23.

64. Cf. Erik H. Erikson, "Memorandum on Youth," *Daedalus*, Summer, 1967, pp. 860–870.

65. Erikson, *Young Man Luther*, p. 14.

66. James, *The Varieties of Religious Experience*, p. 164.

67. Erikson, *Young Man Luther*, p. 41.

68. *Ibid.*, p. 42.

69. Albert Camus, *The Rebel* (Vintage Books, Inc., 1954), pp. 13 ff.

70. Reich, *op. cit.*, pp. 137 ff.

71. Jourard, *op. cit.*, p. 312.

72. Erikson, *Identity, Youth and Crisis*, p. 130.

73. Cf. Pierre Teilhard de Chardin, *The Future of Man* (Harper & Row, Publishers, Inc., 1964), pp. 37 ff.

74. James, *The Varieties of Religious Experience*, p. 173.

75. Erikson, *Young Man Luther*, p. 264.

76. Roszak, *op. cit.*, pp. 206–207.

77. Erich Fromm, *Marx's Concept of Man* (Frederick Ungar Publishing Company, 1966), p. 45. See also Francis Bacon, *Novum Organum*, Aphorisms, Book I, xxxviii ff.

78. John A. T. Robinson, *Honest to God* (The Westminster Press, 1963), p. 125.

79. Dewey, *op. cit.*, p. 9.

80. Karl Rahner, S.J., *Encounters with Silence* (The Newman Press, 1964), pp. 35, 36–37.

81. Fyodor Dostoevsky, *The Brothers Karamazov*, II, 5, Ch. 5, in Fyodor Dostoevsky, *Notes from Underground and The Grand Inquisitor*, tr. by R. E. Matlaw (E. P. Dutton & Company, Inc., 1960), pp. 124–125.

82. Cf. Lepp, *op. cit.*, pp. 153–154.

83. Cf. Hans Urs von Balthasar, "Théologie et Sancteté," *Dieu Vivant*, Vol. XII (1948), pp. 15–31.

84. Butler, *op. cit.*, pp. 127–128.

85. Philip H. Phenix, *Education and the Worship of God* (The Westminster Press, 1966), p. 18.

86. Cf. Martin Buber, *I and Thou* (Charles Scribner's Sons, 1958), pp. 6–8; Mircea Eliade, *The Sacred and the Profane*

(Harper Torchbooks, 1961), pp. 12–13.

87. The main line of argument I have followed here is a reconstruction of the argument against "pure" tolerance that Herbert Marcuse presents in his essay "Repressive Tolerance," in *A Critique of Pure Tolerance,* by Robert Paul Wolff, Barrington Moore, Jr., and Herbert Marcuse (Beacon Press, Inc., 1969).

The logic of this argument is greatly misunderstood, even by enlightened scholars. See, e.g., the following excerpt from a discussion between Robert Coles, a Harvard psychiatrist, and Father Daniel Berrigan, S.J., as it was printed in *Time,* March 22, 1971, p. 17. Referring to the position taken by Berrigan vis-à-vis the tactics of the Weathermen, Coles said the following: "This issue is a very important point, and I find it extremely difficult to deal with because—in my opinion and I'll say it—you're getting close to a position that Herbert Marcuse and others take: you feel that *you* have the right to decide what to 'understand' and by implication to be tolerant of, even approve, and what to condemn strongly or call 'dangerous' at a given historical moment. You feel *you* have the right to judge what is a long-term ideological trend, and what isn't, and you also are judging one form of violence as temporary and perhaps cathartic and useful or certainly understandable, with the passions not necessarily being condoned, whereas another form of violence you rule out as automatically ideological. It isn't too long a step from that to a kind of elitism, if you'll forgive the expression—to an elitism that Marcuse exemplifies, in which he condones a self-selected group who have power and force behind them, who rule and outlaw others in the name of, presumably, the 'better world' that they advocate. There is something there that I find very arrogant and self-righteous and dangerous."

Four points must be briefly noted here. The four are deeply interconnected. (1) The logic of the arguments of Berrigan and Marcuse—and, for that matter, Dewey and Plato, who were not Marxists—arguments, incidentally, with which I totally agree, is that whenever goals are pursued, pure tolerance/pure neutrality is impossible. Having a certain, specific end in view entails the exclusion of certain means that would either not be conducive to the ends or would be positively inimical to them. This is a point of logic that, so it seems, is difficult to comprehend. In other words, there are connections between ends and means such that he who wishes certain ends must wish certain means, or at least not wish certain means. (2) The *"you"* that Coles employs refers to Berrigan and Co. But Coles fails to see that *logically* the *"you"* applies to any and everyone who has ends in view. The Pentagon, for example, has certain ends in view; therefore it must logically exclude ($=$ repress) certain means (such as dissent in the ranks, questioning of orders, curtailment of expenditures). The President has certain ends (political) in view; therefore he must logically exclude ($=$ repress) certain means (such as full truth and candor, true human concerns, true bipartisan cooperation, etc.). Repressive tolerance must be logically exercised by whoever wants to obtain efficaciously certain specific ends.

(3) The *"you"* that Coles employs raises another question. He seems to say, Who are *you* to decide what ought to be pursued, and in relation to which one ought not to be tolerant/neutral? In other words, who sets the goals toward which society *must* conspire? In a democratic society the answer is, of course, the people. But here a problem arises. The people do not have the collective wisdom required to plot humanistic courses. Hence the danger of elitism, to which Coles alludes. In fact, Coles is *so* right, but he fails to open his eyes wide enough. When the Supreme Court decides that "separate but equal" schooling facilities are unconstitutional, their decision *is* elitist, since a very, very small number of people decide for the immense majority. But their decision is based on certain goals which society has decided upon, and which are contained in the Constitution. What the Court does is to establish that certain means (such as segregation) do

not logically conspire toward those ends. In other words, Coles fails to realize that elitism is, in fact, operative in our society today, and that it cannot but be operative, given the fact of the Constitution. Given the *logic* of the argument, therefore, Coles's question should be equally addressed to the Pentagon, the President, the Weathermen, the Klansmen, and the Berrigans.

(4) Finally, one must realize that the logic invoked here is the fundamental basis for *all* "classical" theories of humanism and humanitarian revolt. To affirm the value of man logically entails the negation, the repression, of whatever threatens man's humanity. See Aristotle, *Politics* V; Locke, *Second Treatise* xix; J. S. Mill, *On Representative Government*, Ch. 8; Karl Marx, *Introduction to the Critique of Hegel's Philosophy of Law*.

88. Roszak, *op. cit.*, p. 250.

89. Cf. John Wilson, *Philosophy and Religion* (Oxford University Press, 1961), pp. 86–87.

90. Roszak, *op. cit.*, p. 230.

91. Reich, *op. cit.*, p. 158.

Chapter 3. Programmatic Pointers: The Schools

1. I am indebted for this fable to Alan R. Cohen, who is completing his Ph.D. in psychology at Hofstra University.

2. Plato, *Apology* 37–38 and 40.

3. I have remarked above about "bad trips" and their possible explanation. Here only a few more words would seem necessary.

Much is made of these "bad trips" and of the terrible consequences that accompany them. This danger must be neither ignored nor minimized. But it must be put in the context and perspective of the risks anyone takes who wants to pursue enlightenment and awareness. What the mystics call "the dark night of the soul" is not a pleasant experience. It is never pleasant to experience "the naked knowing and feeling

of their own being," as *The Cloud of Unknowing* puts it.
Gerard Manley Hopkins describes it as a hellish feeling:

> I am gall, I am heartburn. God's most deep decree
> Bitter would have me taste: my taste was me;
> Bones built in me, flesh filled, blood brimmed the curse.
>   Selfyeast of spirit a dull dough sours. I see
> The lost are like this, and their scourge to be
> As I am mine, their sweating selves; but worse.

Teresa of Ávila, in what must be one of the worst "trips" ever
taken by a human being, writes that she felt as if she were
in hell: "I was at prayer one day when suddenly, without
knowing how, I found myself, as I thought, plunged right into
hell. . . . I felt a fire within my soul the nature of which I
am utterly incapable of describing. My bodily sufferings were
so intolerable that, though in my life I have endured the most
severe sufferings of the kind . . . none of them is of the
smallest account by comparison with what I felt then, to say
nothing of the knowledge that they would be endless and
never-ceasing. And even these are nothing by comparison
with the agony of my soul, an oppression, a suffocation and
distressing misery, that I cannot too forcibly describe it. To
say that it is as if the soul were continually being torn from
the body is very little, for that would mean that one's life
was being taken by another; whereas in this case it is the
soul itself that is tearing itself to pieces." (*Life,* Ch. 32.)

   4. Hoffer and Osmond, *op. cit.,* p. 133.

   5. Geller and Boas, *op. cit.,* p. 195.

   6. *Ibid.,* p. 201.

   7. Roszak, *op. cit.,* p. 234.

   8. Geller and Boas, *op. cit.,* p. 190.

   9. Roszak, *op. cit.,* p. 235.

   10. John Dewey, "The School and Society," Part III, in
Martin S. Dworkin (ed.), *Dewey on Education. Selections*
(Teachers College, Columbia University, 1959), pp. 76–78.

   11. John Dewey, "Ethical Principles Underlying Educa-

tion," in Y. Pai and J. T. Myers (eds.), *Philosophic Problems and Education* (J. B. Lippincott Company, 1967), p. 397.

12. Buber, *Between Man and Man,* pp. 10–11.

13. Cf. Peter L. Berger, *A Rumor of Angels* (Doubleday & Company, Inc., 1969), pp. 61 ff.

14. Phenix, *op. cit.,* pp. 28–29.

15. Berger, *op. cit.,* p. 121.

16. Martin Heidegger, *An Introduction to Metaphysics* (Doubleday & Company, Inc., Anchor Books, 1961), p. 77.

17. Otto, *op. cit.,* p. 60.

18. Phenix, *op. cit.,* p. 29.

19. *Ibid.,* p. 23.

20. George B. Leonard, *Education and Ecstasy* (Dell Publishing Company, Inc., 1968), p. 110.

21. Michael Murphy, "Education for Transcendence," in Herbert W. Richardson and Donald R. Cutler (eds.), *Transcendence* (Beacon Press, Inc., 1969), pp. 19–20.

22. Plato, *Epistle* VII. 341 c–d.

23. Cicero, *De amicitia* 23. Cf. Buber, "Education," in *Between Man and Man.*

24. Plato, *Ion* 534 *fine.*

25. Aristotle, *Eudemian Ethics* VII. 14. 1248ᵇ 1.

26. Cf. Ignacio L. Götz, "Inalienable Education," *The Journal of Negro Education,* Vol. XXXIX, No. 4 (Fall, 1970), pp. 278–288; R. E. L. Masters and Jean Houston, *The Varieties of Psychedelic Experience* (Dell Publishing Company, Inc., 1966), pp. 132 ff.

27. Masters and Houston, *op. cit.,* p. 132.

28. *Ibid.,* p. 136.

29. Dr. Houston describes her techniques in some detail in Masters and Houston, *op. cit.,* pp. 134–136. See also the account of one such meaningful experience in *Time,* Oct. 5, 1970, pp. 72–74.

30. Murphy, *loc. cit.,* p. 18.

31. Buber, *Between Man and Man,* pp. 10–11.

32. Plato, *Republic* VII. 514.

33. Jonathan Swift, *Gulliver's Travels,* III. 2.

34. Plato, *Republic* VII. 515.

35. Salvador de Madariaga, "The Dangerous Lure of Parrotland," *Saturday Review,* April 22, 1967, p. 17.

36. Henri Bergson, *Creative Evolution* (Henry Holt & Company, Inc., 1911), p. 165.

37. Plato, *Theaetetus* 155; Aristotle, *Metaphysics* I. 2. 982^b 12 ff.

38. Cf. Martin Heidegger, *What Is Philosophy?* (Twayne Publishers, Inc., 1958), pp. 81 ff.

39. De Madariaga, *op. cit.,* p. 18.

40. Buber, *I and Thou,* p. 7.

41. Pierre Teilhard de Chardin, "On Looking at a Cyclotron," in *Activation of Energy* (Harcourt Brace Jovanovich, 1971), p. 356.

42. Johannes Kepler, *The Harmonies of the World,* V. 7 *fine.*

43. Plato, *Republic* VII. 518.

44. Buber, *Between Man and Man,* pp. 90 ff.

45. "The Unaccountable Element in Science," in Marjorie Grene (ed.), *Knowing and Being: Essays by Michael Polanyi* (The University of Chicago Press, 1969), pp. 117–118; *The Tacit Dimension* (Doubleday & Company, Inc., Anchor Books, 1967), pp. 13 ff.; see also James, *The Varieties of Religious Experience,* p. 298.

46. At times I feel greatly tempted to agree with Norman O. Brown's contention that scientific positivism is a matter of envy. "Mysteries," he writes, "are unpublishable because only some can see them, not all. Mysteries are intrinsically esoteric, and as such an offense to democracy: is not publicity a democratic principle? Publication makes it republican—a thing of the people. The pristine academies were esoteric and aristocratic, self-consciously separate from the profane vulgar. Democratic resentment denies that there can be anything that can't be seen by everybody; in the democratic academy, truth is subject to public verification; truth

is what any fool can see. This is what is meant by the so-called scientific method: so-called science is the attempt to democratize knowledge—the attempt to substitute method for insight, mediocrity for genius by getting an operating procedure. The great equalizers dispensed by the scientific method are the tools, those analytical tools. The miracle of genius is replaced by the standardized mechanism. But fools with tools are still fools." (Norman O. Brown, "Apocalypse: The Place of Mystery in the Life of the Mind," in Mitchell Goodman (ed.), *The Movement Toward a New America,* p. 629; Alfred A. Knopf, Inc., 1970.)

47. Phenix, *op. cit.,* pp. 28–29.

48. Harry S. Broudy, "On 'Knowing With,' " in *Proceedings of the Philosophy of Education Society,* 1970, p. 102.

EPILOGUE

1. Roszak, *op. cit.,* p. 159.

BIBLIOGRAPHY

BIBLIOGRAPHY

Allport, Gordon W., *The Individual and His Religion*. The Macmillan Company, 1960.

Balthasar, Hans Urs von, "Théologie et Sancteté," *Dieu Vivant*, Vol. XII (1948), pp. 15–31.

Barber, Theodore X., *LSD, Marijuana, Yoga, and Hypnosis*. Aldine Publishing Company, 1970.

Berger, Peter L., *A Rumor of Angels*. Doubleday & Company, Inc., 1969.

Bergson, Henri, *Creative Evolution*. Henry Holt & Company, Inc., 1911.

——, *The Two Sources of Morality and Religion*. Doubleday & Company, Inc., Anchor Books, 1935.

Berne, Eric, *Games People Play*. Grove Press, Inc., 1964.

Bourke, Vernon J., *Aquinas' Search for Wisdom*. Bruce Publishing Company, 1965.

Braden, William, *The Private Sea: LSD and the Search for God.* Quadrangle Books, Inc., 1967.

Broudy, Harry S., "On 'Knowing With,' " *Proceedings of the Philosophy of Education Society,* 1970, pp. 89–103.

Brown, Norman O., "Apocalypse: The Place of Mystery in the Life of the Mind," in Mitchell Goodman (ed.), *The Movement Toward a New America.* Alfred A. Knopf, Inc., 1970, pp. 628–630.

Buber, Martin, *I and Thou.* Charles Scribner's Sons, 1958.

——, *Between Man and Man.* The Macmillan Company, 1965.

Butler, Dom Cuthbert, *Western Mysticism.* 2d ed.; Harper Torchbooks, 1966.

Camus, Albert, *The Myth of Sisyphus.* Vintage Books, Inc., 1955.

——, *The Rebel.* Vintage Books, Inc., 1954.

Castaneda, Carlos, *The Teachings of Don Juán: A Yaqui Way of Knowledge.* Ballantine Books, 1968.

Clark, Walter Houston, *Chemical Ecstasy: Psychedelic Drugs and Religion.* Sheed & Ward, Inc., 1969.

Conwell, Joseph F., S.J., *Contemplation in Action.* Gonzaga University Press, 1957.

Cosgriff, Thomas M., "The Problem of Drug Abuse," *Notre Dame Journal of Education,* Vol. I, No. 4 (Winter, 1971).

Delgado, José M. R., *Emotions.* Wm. C. Brown Company, 1966.

Dewey, John, *A Common Faith.* Yale University Press, 1968.

——, "The School and Society," in Martin S. Dworkin (ed.), *Dewey on Education. Selections.* Teachers College, Columbia University, 1959.

——, "Ethical Principles Underlying Education," in Y. Pai and J. T. Myers (eds.), *Philosophic Problems and Education.* J. B. Lippincott Company, 1967.

Dostoevsky, Fyodor, *Notes from Underground and The Grand Inquisitor.* E. P. Dutton & Company, Inc., 1960.

Ducasse, Paul, *A Philosophical Scrutiny of Religion.* The

Ronald Press Company, 1953.

Dworkin, Martin S. (ed.), *Dewey on Education. Selections.* Teachers College, Columbia University, 1959.

Eliade, Mircea, *The Sacred and the Profane.* Harper Torchbooks, 1961.

Erikson, Erik H., *Childhood and Society.* 2d ed.; W. W. Norton & Company, Inc., 1963.

———, *Young Man Luther.* W. W. Norton & Company, Inc., 1958.

———, *Identity, Youth and Crisis.* W. W. Norton & Company, Inc., 1968.

———, "Memorandum on Youth," *Daedalus,* Summer, 1967.

Freemantle, Anne, *The Protestant Mystics.* London: George Weidenfeld & Nicolson, Ltd., 1964.

Fromm, Erich, *Man for Himself.* Fawcett World Library, 1967.

———, *Psychoanalysis and Religion.* Yale University Press, 1967.

———, *Marx's Concept of Man.* Frederick Ungar Publishing Company, 1966.

Geller, Allen, and Boas, Maxwell, *The Drug Beat.* Cowles Book Company, Inc., 1969.

Goodman, Mitchell (ed.), *The Movement Toward a New America.* Alfred A. Knopf, Inc., 1970.

Götz, Ignacio L., "Inalienable Education," *The Journal of Negro Education,* Vol. XXXIX, No. 4 (Fall, 1970), pp. 278–288.

Grene, Marjorie (ed.), *Knowing and Being: Essays by Michael Polanyi.* The University of Chicago Press, 1969.

Heidegger, Martin, *An Introduction to Metaphysics.* Doubleday & Company, Inc., Anchor Books, 1961.

———, *What Is Philosophy?* Twayne Publishers, Inc., 1958.

Hoffer, Abram, and Osmond, Humphrey, *The Hallucinogens.* Academic Press, Inc., 1967.

Houston, Jean, "Psycho-Chemistry and the Religious Consciousness," *International Philosophical Quarterly,* Vol. V

152   BIBLIOGRAPHY

(Spring, 1965), pp. 397–413.

Huxley, Aldous, *The Doors of Perception*. London: Chatto & Windus, Ltd., 1954.

——, "Readings in Mysticism," in Christopher Isherwood (ed.), *Vedanta*. London: George Allen & Unwin, Ltd., 1948.

Isherwood, Christopher (ed.), *Bhagavad-Gita*. The New American Library, Inc., Mentor Books, 1944.

—— (ed.), *Vedanta*. London: Chatto & Windus, Ltd., 1954.

James, William, *The Varieties of Religious Experience*. The New American Library, Inc., Mentor Books, 1958.

——, "The Sentiment of Rationality," in Alburey Castell (ed.), *William James, Essays in Pragmatism*. Hafner Pub. Co., Inc., 1948.

Jourard, Sidney M., "Psychedelic Drugs and the Young: A Social-Phenomenological View," *Notre Dame Journal of Education*, Vol. I, No. 4 (Winter, 1971).

Klüver, Heinrich, *Mescal and Mechanisms of Hallucinations*. The University of Chicago Press, 1966.

Kytle, Jack, "Better Living Through Chemistry?" *Outside the Net*, No. 1 (Winter, 1970), pp. 12–13.

Leary, Timothy F., and Clark, Walter H., "Religious Implications of Consciousness Expanding Drugs," *Religious Education*, Vol. LVIII, No. 2 (May, 1963).

Leonard, George B., *Education and Ecstasy*. Dell Publishing Company, Inc., 1968.

Lepp, Ignace, *Atheism in Our Time*. The Macmillan Company, 1964.

Madariaga, Salvador de, "The Dangerous Lure of Parrotland," *Saturday Review*, April 22, 1967.

Marcuse, Herbert, "Repressive Tolerance," in *A Critique of Pure Tolerance*, by Robert Paul Wolff, Barrington Moore, Jr., and Herbert Marcuse. Beacon Press, Inc., 1969.

Marin, Peter, and Cohen, Allan Y., *Understanding Drug Use: An Adult's Guide to Drugs and the Young*. Harper & Row, Publishers, Inc., 1971.

Masters, R. E. L., and Houston, Jean, *The Varieties of Psychedelic Experience*. Dell Publishing Company, Inc., 1966.

Michaelsen, Robert, "The Public Schools and 'America's Two Religions,'" *Journal of Church and State,* Vol. VIII (Autumn, 1966), pp. 380–400.

Murphy, Michael, "Education for Transcendence," in Herbert W. Richardson and Donald R. Cutler (eds.), *Transcendence*. Beacon Press, Inc., 1969.

O'Dea, Thomas F., *The Sociology of Religion*. Prentice-Hall, Inc., 1966.

Otto, Rudolf, *The Idea of the Holy*. Galaxy Books, 1958.

Pahnke, Walter N., and Richards, William A., "Implications of LSD and Experimental Mysticism," *Journal of Religion and Health,* Vol. V (1966).

Paissac, H., O.P., "Athéisme chez les chrétiens," *Vie Spirituelle, Supplement,* I (1947), pp. 5–28.

Pai, Young, and Myers, J. T. (eds.), *Philosophic Problems and Education*. J. B. Lippincott Company, 1967.

Phenix, Philip H., *Education and the Worship of God*. The Westminster Press, 1966.

Polanyi, Michael, *The Tacit Dimension*. Doubleday & Company, Inc., Anchor Books, 1967.

Rahner, Karl, S.J., *Encounters with Silence*. The Newman Press, 1964.

Reich, Charles A., *The Greening of America*. Random House, Inc., 1970.

Richardson, Herbert W., and Cutler, Donald R. (eds.), *Transcendence*. Beacon Press, Inc., 1969.

Robinson, John A. T., *Honest to God*. The Westminster Press, 1963.

Roszak, Theodore, *The Making of a Counter Culture*. Doubleday & Company, Inc., 1969.

Smith, David E. (ed.), *Drug Abuse Papers 1969*. 2d ed.; Berkeley: Continuing Education in Criminology, University Extension, University of California, 1969.

Smith, Huston, "Do Drugs Have Religious Import?" *Journal*

of Philosophy, Vol. LXI, No. 18 (1964), pp. 517–530.

Spinks, G. Stephens, *Psychology and Religion.* Beacon Press, Inc., 1963.

Stace, Walter T., *Mysticism and Philosophy.* J. B. Lippincott Company, 1960.

Suzuki, Daisetz T., *The Essentials of Zen Buddhism.* London: Rider & Co., 1962.

Teilhard de Chardin, Pierre, *Activation of Energy.* Harcourt Brace Jovanovich, Inc., 1971.

——, *The Future of Man.* Harper & Row, Publishers, Inc., 1964.

——, *Hymn of the Universe.* Harper & Row, Publishers, Inc., 1965.

Wach, Joachim, *Types of Religious Experience, Christian and Non-Christian.* The University of Chicago Press, 1951.

Watts, Alan, *The Book. On the Taboo Against Knowing Who You Are.* Collier Books, 1966.

——, *The Joyous Cosmology.* Vintage Books, Inc., 1962.

Wescott, Malcolm R., *Toward a Contemporary Psychology of Intuition.* Holt, Rinehart and Winston, Inc., 1968.

Wilson, John, *Philosophy of Religion.* London: Oxford University Press, 1961.